VICTIM ASSISTANCE HANDBOOK

Margaret L. Brown
Rowan University

Stanley B. Yeldell
Rowan University

KENDALL/HUNT PUBLISHING COMPANY
4050 Westmark Drive   Dubuque, Iowa 52002

DEDICATION OF LOVE AND LIFE

This Victim Assistance Handbook is dedicated to my belated father, Harry F. Brown who throughout his life has loved and helped people under trying and devastating circumstances. This book is also dedicated to my belated grandmother, Margaret Edelman-Brown and my mother, Margaret Callum-Brown, who through their elderly years have taught me their wisdom and spiritual being.

DEDICATION OF INSPIRATIONS

This handbook is dedicated to my belated mother, Bernice Yeldell who never grew tired of sharing and giving to those in need. Her life will serve as the cornerstone for generations to come and especially for those who are searching for the courage to stand tall during adverse times.

Moreover, may this text serve as a living testimony to my wife, Shirley J. Yeldell, who always inspires me to complete this manuscript with a sense of commitment to the numerous victims of society.

Furthermore, may this text serve as a reminder to my great nieces, Jordyn Young, Danielle and Cierra Champion, and Billie Sumiel and my great nephews; Brandon and Donavon Yeldell, and Nicolas Sumiel that your dreams can be enhanced by always believing that God is the author and finisher of your faith.

Finally, may this text serve as a reminder to my aunts, Henrietta Carter and Lois Pritchett and my uncle, Fred Carter that mom's life articulated the true spirit in providing service to the forgotten victims.

CONTENTS

ACKNOWLEDGMENTS

We would like to personally express our appreciation to the criminal justice professional, and criminal justice students who have contributed to this handbook, which is richer because of their personal sharing:

Robert Schwartz, Deputy Chief of the Atlantic City Police Department, Vice President of the Board of Directors of the Atlantic County Women's Center, and an adjunct professor of the Law and Justice Studies Department of Rowan University, NJ

Heather Van Kleef, a recent graduate of the Law and Justice Studies Department and a Student Research Assistant for the Law and Justice Studies Department of Rowan University, NJ

Jennifer Walters, Psychology Department student and Research Assistant for the Law and Justice Studies Department

PREFACE

The Victimology Course is a very interesting and diverse vehicle for providing students the opportunity to examine the numerous problems crime victims must encounter in response to the judiciary and the policymakers.

Our interest in this handbook evolved from teaching the victimology course over a duration of twenty-five or more years within the Law and Justice Studies Department at Rowan University. We have discovered there was more than ample need to design and craft a text targeted for criminal justice students and related students who study the ever evolving field of victimology.

Our goal is to formulate and develop a handbook in which each chapter is very simplistic and comprehensive; so as to expedite the learning process without the entailment of mundane jargons. Also, the handbook invites the student to actively participate within the learning process rather than the consumption by passive osmosis.

It is believed that the American criminal justice system has been said to be a set of scales with the accused on one side and the victim on the other. Many victims and their advocates argue that there should be a balance of rights between the involved diverse parties. The insuring of these rights of one without infringing on the rights of the other is the central problem and many legal rights experts say a victims rights amendment will not resolve the numerous problems. However, the proponents of such amendments say they don't want to scale back defendant's rights; they simply want victims to have the chance to correct the wrongs against them.

How and why did the American criminal justice system grow in such a way that many people believe in the need for the victims' rights? As the rights for victims expand, what effects are there on the system?

Finally, the handbook seeks to provide an understanding of the impact of the criminal justice field with a foundation for grasping the complexities of criminal victimization.

CHAPTER ONE

INTRODUCTION

This handbook will provide the student with a concise examination of the ever changing field of victimology. The handbook will serve as a very practical and resourceful text that includes simplistic concepts coupled with numerous victim assistance programs.

Each chapter reveals the authors understanding of the integral obstacles that victims entail. The literature has been presented so that the students will be able to glean the victim relationship with the criminal justice system.

Although, less than exhaustive in its treatment of the various issues, the handbook's broad treatment of the major problems confronted by crime victims and the signs and symptoms enhances the utility of the text. It includes a meaty description of prevention solutions embellished within the context of the handbook and the internet network diverse sources.

The handbook consists of twenty readable and informative chapters that have been well positioned to articulate the prevailing subjects within the field of victimology. The handbook commences with **Chapter One: The Introduction** presents the theme of the book, with particular attention to the broad subject matter coupled with the preventative methods that are available for the victim; **Chapter Two:** addresses the **Victim Rights** as being fundamental within the reform efforts of the United States and State Constitutions by adding victim-oriented provisions; **Chapter Three: Victim Assistance** introduces the student to the numerous victim assistance services that may be pursued by the victim; **Chapter Four: Educational Requirements** which articulates the victimology course syllabus and its required assignments; **Chapter Five: Restitution From Offenders** holds the offender partially or fully accountable for the financial losses suffered by the crime victims; **Chapter Six: Civil Remedies:** provides the injuried party with the avenues that may be pursued in civil court for financial redress; **Chapter Seven: Insurance Programs:** was formulated to introduce the victim to the various types of insurance programs that may reimburse or repay the crime victims for his or her losses; **Chapter Eight: Victim Compensation Programs** will focus on polices and procedures that are mandated by state and federal guidelines and the victim assistance funding opportunities; **Chapter Nine: Victims of Murder** will be able to ascertain the vital concepts of this chapter as it relates to defining the criminal homicides to survivors patterns and how they differ in response to the homicide event; **Chapter Ten: Kidnapping and Abductions of Children** and the reduction of risks; **Chapter Eleven: Victims of Child Abuse** of children will focus on kidnapping and abductions and the reductions of risks; **Chapter Eleven: Victims of Child Abuse:** attempts to differentiate between abuse and neglect and the various types of abuse the victim encounters; **Chapter Twelve: Victims of Elder Abuse** explains who the elderly are and how to prevent and respond to elder abuse, neglect, exploitation and related offenses: **Chapter Thirteen: Victims of Spouse Abuse** will articulate the violence found between husbands and wives or other conjugal cohabitants and the cycle of violence theory; **Chapter Fourteen: Victim Assistance - Sexual Assaults** will examine the major theories that purport to texplain why rape occurs and analyze the rape trauma syndrome and the Megan Law; **Chapter Fifteen: Victim Assistance - Stalking** introduces the student to the stalker behavior, categories used to classify stalking cases, the method and motives of stalkers and strategies that can be utilized by the victims: **Chapter Sixteen: Victim Assistance - Drunk Driving** informs the student that drunk driving is the most frequently committed violent crime in the United States and it will reveal the prevention strategies that are recommended: **Chapter Seventeen: Restorative Justice and Reconciliation** enhances the student's comprehensive of the victim-offender reconciliation programs and explains the importance of restorative justice as an alternative in achieving closure for the victim; **Chapter Eighteen: Trends and Visions** has been designed to examine the trends in the field of victimology and especially the retaliatory justice concept plus the identification of vigilantism and emergence of church abuse; **Chapter Nineteen: Grants** will supplement the students knowledge of the vast directory of grants that may be pursued as articulated by the office for victims of crime of the United States Department of Justice: and **Chapter Twenty: Directory of Victim Assistance Programs** are designed to inform the students of the victim assistance programs commencing from the State of Alabama and ending with the State of Wyoming.

CHAPTER TWO

VICTIM RIGHTS

INTRODUCTION

This chapter will address the rights that victims have achieved during the last decade. It commences with a discussion of the fundamental rights of the victim and the efforts to reform the United States and State Constitutions by adding victim-oriented provisions.

A prominent playing field has been the issue of victim impact statements. The last theme developed, introduces the student to the alternatives involved with the informal victim participation.

A. CHAPTER OUTLINE:

1) Fundamental Rights for Victim
2) Victims Notification
3) Present Throughout All Proceedings
4) Victim Consultation with Prosecutor or The District Attorney
5) Right to be Heard
6) Right to Reasonable Protection
7) Mandatory Restitution
8) Right to Disposition of Proceedings Without Any Delays or Postponement
9) Right to Full Range of Services and Support Assistance
10) Fundamental Rights Enforced in All Juvenile Proceedings
11) Criminal and Juvenile Justice Agencies Should Ensure Victims Receive Information That They can Understand
12) Advocates Should be Available to Assist Victims
13) Prohibit Advise Action Against Victims
14) Victims Should be Tested for HIV Virus and Sexually Transmitted Diseases
15) Community Impact Statements
16) Conclusion
17) Required Assignment

THE VICTIM RIGHTS

1) FUNDAMENTAL RIGHTS

The rights described within this section are among the most significant. The right to notice of all criminal proceedings and to attend them, to make a statement to the court regarding bail, sentencing, and any knowledge about plea-bargains. The right to speak at parole hearings.

2) VICTIM NOTIFICATION

The right for crime victims to be notified regarding criminal proceedings in a timely fashion is fundamental to their exercise of other rights. Victims should have the right to be notified of any significant change in the status of the defendant's case.

3) PRESENT THROUGHOUT ALL PROCEEDINGS

Victims should have the right to be present throughout all criminal court proceedings. Technology offers increasingly powerful tools for providing immediate notification to crime victims. The victim should not exclude when he or she will become a major participating witness in the criminal proceeding.

4) VICTIM CONSULTATION

The prosecutor or District Attorney should provide victims an opportunity for meaningful consultation prior to the major case decision such as the dismissal. The prosecutor or District Attorney should provide reasonable explanations of the criminal justice system and its critical stages that will be encountered by the victim.

5) THE RIGHT TO BE HEARD

The crime victims should have the right to be heard in major criminal proceedings including the:

     a) Pretrial Hearings
     b) Bail Hearings
     c) Sentencing
     d) Prior to Plea Agreements
     e) Probation
     f) Parole

The input can be written or audio taped statements. Allowing the victim to be heard on the issue of pretrial release helps to inform the court regarding the degree of danger posed by a defendant.

6) THE RIGHT TO REASONABLE PROTECTION

The victim and witness of crime should have the right to reasonable protection, including, protection from intimidation. The safety of the victim and witness should be paramount when determining whether offenders should be released from custody.

7) MANDATORY RESTITUTION

Orders of full restitution for crime victims should be mandatory. Restitution orders should be automatically entered as civil judgments at the end of the offender's supervisory period if not paid.

8) THE RIGHT TO DISPOSITION

The victims should have the right to disposition of proceedings free from unreasonable delay. The victim should not endure hardships and trauma due to repeated delays or postponements.

9) THE RIGHT TO FULL RANGE OF SERVICES AND SUPPORT ASSISTANCE

The crime victims must have a full range of services and support assistance to enable them to recover physically, psychologically, and in practical ways from the effects of crime.

10) FUNDAMENTAL RIGHTS ENFORCED IN ALL JUVENILE PROCEEDINGS

The rights of victims of juvenile offenders should mirror the rights of victims of adult offenders. Victims of juvenile offenders should have the right to provide input through victim impact statements.

11) CRIMINAL AND JUVENILE JUSTICE AGENCIES SHOULD ENSURE THAT VICTIMS RECEIVE INFORMATION THAT THEY CAN UNDERSTAND

The justice system and professionals should provide explanations of the victim's rights in writing. The explanations of rights and services should be reinforced by all justice personnel and victim service providers.

12) ADVOCATES SHOULD BE AVAILABLE TO ASSIST VICTIMS

The advocates should be available to explain rights to victims and help them exercise those rights whenever necessary, especially when the victims are underage on incapacitated.

13) PROHIBIT ADVICE ACTIONS AGAINST VICTIMS

The Federal and State laws should prohibit employers from turning advise actions against victims who must be absent from work so they can participate in the criminal justice process.

14) VICTIMS SHOULD BE TESTED FOR HIV VIRUS AND SEXUALLY TRANSMITTED DISEASES

In cases where there is good cause to believe that bodily fluids were exchanged, victims should have the right to be tested and to have the accused or convicted offender tested at appropriate times for the HIV virus and the sexually transmitted diseases.

15) COMMUNITY IMPACT STATEMENTS

Criminal justice agencies should facilitate community impact statements as a means for members of a neighborhood or community that has been impacted by crime to have input into sentencing.[1]

SUMMARY

A significant number of victim rights advocates argue that having victims play a more important part of the criminal justice system is both empowering and therapeutic.

The crime victims would be more empowered because they, instead of the prosecutor would decide whether to bring suit or settle a case. It would be better for society to accommodate crime victim's rights in a court system designed to resolve disputes between individuals, rather than awkwardly attaching duties and structures to serve individual needs to a court process created and evolved to serve societal needs.

CHAPTER THREE

VICTIM ASSISTANCE

INTRODUCTION

During the early 1960's the seriousness of crime commenced to increase in the United States and its impact on American life became evident by the 1970's. In 1981, prior to the formation of the President's Task Force on Victim of Crime, a vast number of individuals were victimized. This substantial elevation of crime launched the victims movement coupled with the need for victim assistance programs.[2]

The first and most important victim assistance programs were borne in 1972. They were the rape crisis programs: Bay Area Woman Against Rape in Alamedia County, California, and the Rape Crisis Services in Washington, D. C.. The second of three was the Aid to Victims of Crime, in St. Louis, Missouri, which specialized in crisis intervention for all crime victims. In 1974, the first battered woman's shelter was established in Denver, Colorado. The victim assistance programs have been designed to provide a broad based of services in the forms of emotional, practical, and related ongoing support system. The chapter will explore some of the essential services that are necessary to enhance the support and guidance of the victim.[3]

The purpose of this chapter is to introduce students to victimization data. The discussion of the victimization data will be concentrated on the leading surveys utilized to measure victimization rates. The surveys will articulate it's importance and shortcomings or weakness.

OBJECTIVES

The victim assistance programs attempted to provide some of the subsequent services:

1. Lessen trauma of victimization
2. Provide short-term emotional support and compassion
3. Assist victims to cope with the impact of crime and/or tragic circumstances
4. Practical assistance
5. Encourage victims to connect with other appropriate service support programs
6. Assist law enforcement agencies in their response to victim needs
7. Educate and promote victim assistance within the community

The victim assistance service programs will be discussed in detail in the following chapter, but examine the subsequent list of services:

1. Partner Abuse
2. Family Crisis
3. Sexual Assault
4. Robbery
5. Fire
6. Property Crime/Damage
7. Homicide Services
8. Sudden Death
9. Accidents
10. Multi Casualty/Disaster
11. Elderly Abuse
12. Death Notification
13. Missing Persons
14. Stalking
15. Victim Compensation

DEFINITION OF CONCEPTS

1. Uniform Crime Report (UCR): Crime statistics compiled and published by the Federal Bureau of Investigation (FBI).

2. National Crime Victimization Survey (NCVS): The Bureau of Justice Statistics records the victims statements and their victimization encounters.

3. Victims of Crime Act of 1984: Created the Federal Crime Victims Fund, and provided a more stable source of funding for local victim assistance programs.

4. Office of Victims of Crime (OVC): Provided financial and technical support for the development and dissemination of model protocols of victim assistance programs.

5. Violence Against Women Grants Office: Assists the National Criminal Justice System in responding to the need and concern of women who have been victimized by violence.

6. National Organization for Victim Assistance (NOVA): The world's oldest broad-based victim rights group. A non-profit membership organization is guided by the purpose of servicing its members.

7. Victim: The individual embraces all those who experience injuries, losses, or hardships due to any and all causes.

8. Victimization: Is a dynamic process that emerges through a series of stages. The stages commence with the risk factors and go through the precipitating condition that result into harmful consequences.

9. Victimology: Is the scientific study of victims, which includes a relationship between the offender, criminal justice system, and the victim.

10. Induces victimization: The concept refers to individuals called: the offender, perpetrator, and oppressor.[4]

STATISTICS OF CRIME

The Uniform Crime Report (UCR) includes the "Crime Clock," which is a report that summarizes the annual crime rate according to fixed intervals.

CRIME CLOCK

The Crime Clock articulates a time line or time computation of violent crime and property crimes and it is measured in seconds and minutes. The time line of crime is representations made by within the UCR data. The data can be found in the FBI Uniform Crime Report. The subsequent made of the time line and it should not be accepted to represent a continued regularity in the commission of the offenses, rather than an annual ratio of crime fixed time intervals:

OFFENSE	TIME
1. Violent Crime	every 19 seconds
2. Murder	every 27 minutes
3. Forcible Rape	every 6 minutes
4. Robbery	every 54 seconds
5. Property Crime	every 3 seconds
6. Burglary	every 12 seconds
7. Larceny or Theft	every 4 seconds
8. Motor Vehicle Theft	every 23 seconds

The Crime Clock should be examined with caution, since the UCR is designed to convey the annual reporting of crime and not the frequency or occurrences of when crime or offenses are committed.[5]

The UCR maintains considerable information about arrests and convictions, including demographic characteristics of apprehended, charged, and convicted persons.

The National Crime Survey (NCVS), a victimization survey, systematically monitors serious crime rates and the characteristics of crime and crime victims. The subjects are interviewed regarding their experiences with crime in a given time period.[6] The seven crimes routinely included on the NCVS are as follows:

1. Assault
2. Burglary
3. Household larceny-theft of property
4. Motor vehicle theft
5. Personal theft
6. Rape
7. Robbery

The NCS does not assess crimes against children, including only persons over age 12 in the survey. Domestic crimes, vandalism, and low-incidence crimes such as murder and arson are also not included and sexual assault is not adequately detect.

SUMMARY

Anyone can be victimized, and anyone may be called on to help a victim. Victims have successfully lived through unfair, demanding life experiences. To be an effective victim assistance service worker, whether as a volunteer or professional, one must understand victimization and how best to support the victim's work toward continued survival and growth.

Public opinion and social attitudes, which change over time, influence those perceptions. Currently, public attention and resources are predominately directed at people who have been hurt by interpersonal acts that could be treated as crimes.

Victimization takes many forms, but common themes can be identified across various types. Special knowledge about such acts as sexual assault, spousal violence, specific crimes, racial discrimination, and child and elder maltreatment is essential for work with victims of those forms of victimization.

Surveys and official reporting systems provide the foundation for estimating the magnitude of victimization and monitoring trends. In general, victimization is common, is increasingly brought to the attention of the criminal justice system, and is as likely to be perpetrated by someone known to the victim as by a stranger. It can happen to anyone, although the poor, minorities, and adolescents/young adults are particularly at risk.

Survey statistics and official reports essentially have different purposes. Surveys attempt to locate cases that are unknown to authorities and detect information that may be too sensitive for disclosure to authorities. Official reporting systems can effectively guide program planning for investigative agencies. Surveys usually detect higher rates than the reporting systems. The findings of surveys and reporting systems are not to be compared as "better or worse" than one another, rather, they are qualitatively different and each yields valuable information.

CHAPTER FOUR

EDUCATIONAL REQUIREMENTS

It has been said that victimology lacks certain theoretical perspectives and foundation. Victimology may represent a different focus of application of theoretical insights already explored by other disciplines, which are essential because of their interest in people being comfortable with crisis.

Individuals who are vulnerable and/or in crisis may indeed constitute the common factor linkage of victimology with other relevant disciplines and providing a focus for intervention.

INTRODUCTION

This chapter is designed to introduce the students to the essential course requirements. The chapter outline will discuss the following:

1) Victimology Syllabus
2) Course Background
3) Course Objectives
4) Required Textbook
5) Evaluations
6) Requirements and Grading
7) Required Readings

CHAPTER OUTLINE

The chapter outline will introduce the students to the course requirements of victimology.

VICTIMOLOGY SYLLABUS

The syllabus will articulate the course requirements and the expectations that must be adhered by the student. The subsequent victimology syllabus serves as an example or working model that maybe utilized by colleges and universities.

1. **Law/Justice Reference Number:**
   a) 21052201
   b) 21052202
Fall/Spring
2. **Schedule:**
   a) TR 9:30 – 10:45 A.M.
   b) W 6:30 – 9:00 P.M.
3. **Credits:** Three (3) credits
4. **Instructor:** Dr. Stanley B. Yeldell
5. **Office Location:** Wilson Building – Room 118
6. **Office Phone:** 1-856-256-4500, ext. 3837 3537
7. **Office Hours:** Monday – 9:00 A.M. to 12:00 Noon

COURSE BACKGROUND

The criminologists and criminal justice professionals have focused a substantial attention upon the offender and the criminal justice system. However, we have seen a new emergence on the other, forgotten member of the criminal dyad: the victim. Some observers might prefer to examine the scientific study of victims as merely another facet or extension of criminology and criminal justice, other scholars have ralley around the emergence of victimology as a long overdue development. The victimological movement includes both, the academicians and practitioners whom have achieved significant hurdles over the past two decades. The purpose of this course is to introduce students to these developments and to the ongoing victim related issues and assistance programs.

COURSE OBJECTIVES

1) To introduce students to the development of the field of victimology;
2) To delineate conceptual boundaries of victimology;
3) To familiarize the student with the basic concepts and literature within the various areas and related of victimology;
4) To explore policy developments and practical applications that stem from the concerns of victim;
5) To introduce the students to the victim rights;
6) To introduce students to the various victim assistance programs;
7) To familiarize the students with civil courts, insurance programs, and their purpose of the victim compensation program;
8) To examine the numerous victim assistance programs and the trend and visions of the fields of victimology.

REQUIRED TEXTBOOK

Victim Assistance Handbook, Brown, Margaret, and Yeldell, Stanley B. Kendall/Hunt Publishing, Co., 2002

EVALUATION

8) Final Examination 100%

REQUIREMENTS AND GRADING

There will be no extensions or make-ups for required research assignments. The due dates will be final unless changed by the professor. The assignments will commence at the end of the following chapters: Five to Seventeen.

The final examination will be required and it will be scheduled at the end of the semester. The failure to take the final examination, you will be awarded an "0" for "F" as for your computation in the evaluation process. Extra-credit projects, such as book reviews or team papers, are not acceptable substitutes for an undesirable grade.

Reasonable accommodations for students with disabilities may be arranged by contacting the instructor on an individual basis during the first week of class.

The student will be required to make mandatory visits to the selected victim assistance centers or programs.

REQUIRED READINGS

Week 1:   Chapters One to Two

Week 2:   Chapters Three to Four

Week 3:   Chapters Five to Six

Week 4:   Chapters Seven to Eight

Week 5:   Chapter Nine

Week 6:   Chapters Ten to Eleven

Week 7:   Chapter Twelve

Week 8:   Chapter Thirteen

Week 9:   Chapter Fourteen

Week 10:   Chapter Fifteen

Week 11:   Chapter Sixteen

Week 12:   Chapter Seventeen

Week 13:   Chapter Eighteen

Week 14:   Review for Final Exam

Week 15:   Review for Final Exam

Week 16:   Final Examination

CHAPTER FIVE

RESTITUTION FROM OFFENDERS

INTRODUCTION

Restitution holds the offenders partially or fully accountable for the financial losses suffered by the victims of their crimes. Restitution is typically ordered in juvenile and criminal courts to compensate victims for out-of-pocket expenses that are the direct result of a crime. Most often, it is ordered in cases of property crime such as home burglary involving stolen or damaged property or the theft of goods from a retail store. However, it may be applied to reimburse victims of violent crime for current and future expenses related to their physical and mental health recovery and to make up for loss of support for survivors of homicide victims.

Restitution is not a punishment or an alternative to fines, or interventions with the offender. It is a debt owed to the victim.

OBJECTIVES

The victims can seek to recover their financial losses in a variety of ways.

1. Making the offender pay is everyone's first choice, as it embodies the most elemental notion of justice.
2. Judges in criminal cases can order the offender to make restitution.
3. Judges and jurors in civil court can compel defendants to pay damages.
4. Grossly negligent third party, such as an enterprise or a governmental agency to bear the responsibility for the criminal incident.
5. Insurance coverage can also be a source of repayment.
6. Financial aid can be fourth coming from state compensation programs that cover certain expenses and losses.

RESTITUTIONAL TERMS

1. Restitution: Is the responsibility of the offender to repay the victim for losses or expenses due to the crime.
2. Compensation: Is the financial obligation of government-run funds or private insurance companies.
3. Community Restitution: Convicted or adjudicated offenders pay back the community through the performance of service.
4. The Court-Ordered Payment System (COPS): The program requires offenders to make payments to the state, which is converted to government checks and distributed to victims and other payees.
5. Civil Judgment: Can be enforced by placing a lien on real property, garnishing wages, attaching assets or wages or freezing bank accounts.
6. Forfeiture Bond: Making offenders forfeit bonds money for restitution obligations.
7. Credit Card Payments: Offenders making payment by using their credit cards.7

HISTORICAL DEVELOPMENT

The concept that offenders should provide restitution to the victims of their criminal or delinquent acts can be traced back thousands of years to the earliest forms of laws governing society. In the Bible, recompense to the victim included not only reimbursing or replacing the victim for what was lost, but additional measures as a guilt offering. Over time, the government took the responsibility for prosecuting crime, and crimes were viewed as committed against the state, not against the victim.

The modern-day restitution emerged in the 1930's with the establishment of penal laws in some states permitting restitution as a part of suspended sentences and probation. Between 1960's and 1970's, a number of restitution initiatives evolved. Federal funding became available in the mid-1970's for the development of restitution programs across the country.

It was not until the 1980's that restitution found new prominence as a critical element of the victim's rights movement.

Restitution as a significant remedy for crime victims was first addressed on the federal level with enactment of the Victim and Witness Protection Act (VWPA) of 1982, which required federal judges to order full restitution in criminal cases or state their reasons for not doing so on the record.

Over a decade later, the importance of restitution was emphasized on the federal level with the enactment of 1994 of the Violent Crime Control and Law Enforcement Act, which made restitution mandatory in cases of sexual assault or domestic violence. In 1996, restitution was made mandatory on the federal level in all violent crime cases and in certain other cases with the passage of the Mandatory Victim Restitution Act.

The Federal Bureau of Prisons created a collection of programs in the late 1980's that many state correctional authorities have copied. Payments can be derived from inmates wages, from prison labor, state and federal income tax refunds, lottery winnings, inheritances, trust accounts, and collateral used for bail. More than half of the states legislatures have passed laws that presume restitution will be imposed on every convict unless the presiding judges offers a compelling reason not to do so.[8]

Yet, the principles underlying offender repayment are deceptively simple. They found good in theory, but the numerous problems occur when they are translated into practice.

PHILOSOPHY OF RESTITUTION

The use of community service obligations as a form of restitution benefiting agencies, organizations, institutions, and entire neighborhoods has drawn criticism as can abuse of judicial activism.

The major argument against reimbursement is that the operations of the criminal justice system are intended to benefit society as a whole, not just the injured party. Other considerations should come first punishing criminals harshly to teach them a lesson and to deter would-be law breakers from following their example, treating offenders in residential programs so that they can be released back as rehabilitated and become productive members of incapacitating dangerous persons by confining them for long periods of time.

Some have been promoting an ancient practice as an additional form of punishment, while others it as a better method of rehabilitation. Other champion of restitution emphasizes its beneficial impact on the financial well being of victims and its potential for resolving interpersonal conflicts. As a result, groups with diverse aims and philosophies are pushing restitution, but are pulling at established programs from different directions.

EVALUATING RESTITUTION PROGRAMS

When criminologists and victimologists evaluate the effectiveness of these programs, the challenge is to properly identify the specific goals and to devise appropriate criteria to measure degrees of success and failure. The victim-oriented goals involve making the injured parties "whole again" by enabling them to collect full reimbursement and regain peace of mind or the restoration of victims psychological well-being and the recovery from emotional stress and trauma.

The offender-oriented goals involve the identification of signs of rehabilitation and lowered recidivism. The system-oriented goals include the reducing of cases processing costs, relieving, taxpayers of the financial burden of compensation , victims, alleviating jail and prison over-crowding through alternative sentences, and improving victim cooperation by providing material incentives to injured parties for participating in the criminal justice process.

Victims who have become impatient and dissatisfied with criminal court-ordered restitution can pursue another avenue for reimbursement: lawsuits in civil court. [9]

SUMMARY

Victims can try to recover their financial losses in different ways. The restitution payments can come directly from the offender's earnings seem to be a fair and appropriate methods of reimbursement and may provide a solid foundation for eventual reconciliation. Restitution may be viewed as an additional penalty but also as a way to sensitize and rehabilitate lawbreakers. However, many victims never receive any money because their offenders are not caught, convicted, and sentenced to restitution, or are unable or unwilling to earn and hand over sufficient funds.

CHAPTER ASSIGNMENT

You are required to interview an individual or corporate victims and complete the Restitution Affidavit Form, which will request the losses incurred by the victim. Also you must complete the Individual Victim Form and the Corporate Victim Form.

This assignment is worth 10 points.

INDIVIDUAL VICTIM

Name: _____

Home Address: _____

_____ Telephone: _____

Work Address: _____

_____ Telephone: _____

Alternate Contact: _____

Address: _____

_____ Telephone: _____

Social Security Number: _____-____-_____   DOB: _____/_____/_____

Driver's License Number _____   State _____

CORPORATE VICTIM

Name: _____

Attention: _____

_____

Address: _____

_____ Telephone: _____

Reference Number: _____

STATE COURT _____

STATE OF _____
      Plaintiff,

DA No. _____

v.

GJ No. _____

_____
      Defendant.

CC No. _____

RESTITUTION AFFIDAVIT

    I have suffered the following loses as a result of the Defendant's crime:

1. TRAVEL EXPENSES ($.32/Mile)....................................$_____
   _____

2. MISSED WORK (pay/hour)..$_____
   _____

3. PROPERTY EXPENSES (replace, repair, clean).....................$_____
   _____

4. MEDICAL EXPENSES (medicine, doctor, hospital, ambulance)....$_____
   _____

5. FUNERAL EXPENSES...$_____
   _____

6. OTHER EXPENSES (itemize)......................................$_____
   _____

                         TOTAL.................$_____

I swear that this Restitution Affidavit is true and correct.

Done this _____ day of _____, 20_____.

_____
       Witness

_____
       Signature

NOTES: _____

_____

_____

CHAPTER SIX

CIVIL REMEDIES

INTRODUCTION

The victims of crime often suffer extensive physical, psychological and financial issues, and they are increasingly looking to the civil justice system for reparations. The tangible costs of crime to victims, such as medical expenses, mental health counseling, and the lost of productivity, are estimated at approximately $100 billion plus annually. The intangible costs are the pain, suffering, and the reduced quality of life victims must endure are even greater than $300 billion annually. However, some victims are compensated through state victim compensation or through restitution ordered as a part of a sentence, which these sources frequently fall short of covering their total losses. Moreover, restitution and state-funded compensation rarely, if ever, compensate victims for the diminished quality of life resulting from continuous pain and suffering. A judgment in a civil suit can provide compensation as well as the searing of important preventative measures that would not result from a criminal case.

OBJECTIVES

1. The injured parties seek financial redress through the civil court.
2. The injured party can launch lawsuits designed to remedy torts (private wrongs) arising from criminal violations.
3. Plaintiffs – victims can sue defendants and win judgment for punitive damages (money) extracted to punish wrongdoers, and deter others.
4. Plaintiffs – victims can sue defendants and receive compensatory damages (to repay actual expenses).
5. Civil remedies empower victims to exercise their rights.
6. Victims can decide to utilize their own lawyer(s) or choose their own to pursue civil actions.
7. Victims will have a voice in the outcome of the civil matter.

DEFINITION OF CONCEPTS

1. Plaintiff: Commences the civil action and is the injured party.
2. Defendant: The wrongdoer in the civil case.
3. Complaint: The actual pleading of the document. The brief statement of the facts and the cause of action.
4. Contingency Fee Basis: The lawyer will accept the case on the theory that a fee is not required to initiate the case, but if the lawyer wins, then a fee will be charged.
5. Preponderance of Evidence: The winning side is the one that presents the more convincing argument.
6. Compensatory Damages: The awarding of damages for actual expenses and losses.
7. Judgments: Are awarded by jury verdicts or by the trial judge.
8. Judgment Proof: The wrongdoer or the perpetrators do not have adequate or sufficient funds or sources to pay the judgment.
9. Third Party: Defendants maybe other parties – individuals, entities, businesses, corporations, institutions, or governmental agencies.10

LITIGATION PROCESS

The civil suits can involve claims for punitive damages as well as compensatory and pecuniary damages. The awards for compensatory damages (repayment of expenses and losses), are supposed to restore victims to their former financial condition. They can receive the monetary equivalent of stolen or vandalized property, wages from missed works, projected future earnings that will not become vested because the injuries inflicted by the offender. The outlays for medical and psychiatric care plus recompense for physical pain and mental suffering, which result from the loss of enjoyment, fright, nervousness, grief, humiliation, and disfigurement. The punitive damages may be awarded by the court to make examples out of violators who deliberately act maliciously, oppressively, and recklessly.

In civil courts, the victims can sue the offenders for various intentional torts: wrongful deaths, which enables the survivors to collect compensation for the loss of a loved one without justification or a legitimate excuse; assault, which covers intentionally threatening acts sufficient to cause fear of immediate bodily harm; battery, which involves intentional, harmful, physical contact that is painful. The previous intentional torts are just brief examples of the various civil suits that the victim may institute.

The civil actions commence when the (victim) plaintiff formally files a complaint, which is referred to as the pleading. This document describes the factual issues couples with the justificational requirements and a summary of the essential facts that create a cause of action that articulates the victim's harm. Moreover, the victim harm presents the direct and proximate cause of result of the defendant (alleged wrongdoer's behavioral conduct). Finally, the injuries and damages sustained require the victim (plaintiff) to make a demand upon the defendant (offender) to compensate said plaintiff for the injuries sustained. The demand for damages concludes the complaint by the articulation of the plaintiff's prayer for compensation. The victim's attorney brings the complaints to civil court and pays the appropriate filing fees and expenses.

A deputy sheriff or a private retained process server must physically hand the written document to the defendant (offender); coupled with the summons requiring a written response or the answer to the complaint. The answer must be completed and tendered to the plaintiff (victim) within the statutory direction or time period. The wrongdoer must submit an answer either by admitting to the charges or allegations or else the contesting of them or the mere denial as a defense or the defendant (offender) may counter suit the plaintiff's case. Prior to trial, the parties will complete the discovery process, which is the plaintiff and defendant exchanging their basic information that will be utilized at trial. The exchanging of information must be completed prior to the actual trial.11

It is the discretion of either party; plaintiff or the defendant can enter into an agreed upon settlement. The settlement must be approved by the court.

However, if a settlement is not reached, then the trial will commence by the modified trial:

1. Selection of the jury
2. Opening statements by plaintiff and defendant
3. Plaintiff's direct examination
4. Defendant's cross examination
5. Plaintiff's redirect examination
6. This can lead to closing arguments by both parties
7. The jury verdict – majority of jurors must vote for either side or party

The previous represents the plaintiff's case and the defendant's will have the same opportunity to present his or her case.

The losing party will have the right to appeal the jury's verdict or any other errors that have prompted adverse decision against the losing party. The appeal is usually brought before a higher court; for instance, an Appeals Court of the State Supreme Court.

Remembering, there is a statute of limitations that must be adhered. The failure to file within the prescribed time limit (torts – 2 years to file suits) will be grounds for the case to be dismissed. Since the plaintiff didn't file the complaint according to the statute of limitations.

COLLECTION OF DAMAGES

The majority of the perpetrators of crime are known to be judgment-proof, victims may not be able to collect from the perpetrator since the offender doesn't or can't pay the appropriate damages that the jury has awarded. The plaintiff – victim must select to sue third party individuals or entities, which a legal duty was breached by said entity or governmental agency. The focal point of the third party action is that the third party is to blame for the plaintiff's – victim's misfortune or injuries sustained.

The victims can prevail if they can prove in civil court that the third party did not act to prevent a reasonably foreseeable crime. To prevail, the attorney must convincingly demonstrate that the defendant chronically disregarded complaints, did not post warnings, chose not to rectify conditions and improve the security, and did not offer the degree of protection expected by the community standards.

What is predictable is that successful third-party lawsuits by the victims against custodial officials and agencies will have a chilling effect on wardens, psychiatrists, parole boards, and others who make decisions regarding confinement versus release.[12]

SUMMARY

Victims can try to recover their financial losses in several different ways. Unfortunately, many victims never receive any money because their offenders are not caught, convicted, and sentenced to restitution, or are unable to earn and hand over sufficient funds.

Victims can attempt to sue their offenders in civil court for compensatory and punitive damages. As plaintiffs, they have a better chance of winning against defendants than in criminal court because the standard of proof – a preponderance of the evidence is easier to satisfy the guilt beyond a reasonable doubt. However, only offenders who are identified and who have substantial exposed assets can be successfully sued. If criminals are not caught or have not tangible assets, victims might be able to launch lawsuits against third parties such as businesses or criminal justice agencies that acted with such gross negligence that innocent parties were targeted by dangerous individuals.

A small number of victims might be able to claim a portion of the money that certain convicts make by cashing in on their notoriety.

CHAPTER SEVEN

INSURANCE PROGRAMS

INTRODUCTION

This chapter is formulated to introduce the victim to the various types of insuranc programs that can frequently and routinely reimburse the crime victim for their loss e positive aspect is that a prudent insured can be repaid without too many impedime providing a formal complaint has been filed with law enforcement. The drawbac that a potential target must have the foreseeable or foresight to purchase insurance pro i in advance and an insurance company must be willing to issue the policy. Some duals or businesses reside in high-crime areas which cause a great deal of difficulty in ding coverage to the individual or business.

OBJECTIVES

The objectives will be articulated by discussing the collection of i ce policies and the various forms of reimbursements. The victims must realize that ms for the coverage must be affordable. There are numerous individuals who ' nvisioned that trials and tribulations as it relates to life's dangers, but they do not have sposable income to pay for the insurance protection. The individuals can protect the es against a wide variety of hazards. The life insurance policies can pay sizable s the survivors of murder victims.

DEFINITION OF CONCEP'

1. Double Indemnity: A clause that the survivors twice as much if the policy holder dies unexpecte m an accident or a criminally inflicted injury.
2. Income Maintenance: Cover t can be purchased to offset lost of earnings and expenses due t' cal bills.
3. Property: Insurance cover e to loss or damages.

CATEGORIES O'   JRANCE

There are various categories of insuranc h may assist in alleviating the losses due to crime. The subsequent categories represen' arious avenues which victims may pursue in order to recover losses.

1. Auto and Boat: over losses imposed by theft, vandalism, and arson.
2. Homeowners er losses due to burglary, some larcenies, or items left on porc' in yards, arson, robbery and especially if the confrontat curs within the dwelling.
3. Robbery nce: Some companies sell robbery insurance that reimbu' sses of valuables; like jewelry, cameras, no matter where the cr' curs.
4. Heal' irance: The policies will allow payments for injuries sus' as a result of criminal incidents.

5. Workmans Compensation Insurance: The coverage of an employee injured while employed.

MISCELLANEOUS COVERAGE

The injured victim may qualify for other and related coverage or compensation, such as filing a disability claim with the State's Disability Fund and, The Federal Supplemental Security Income Fund. The injured victim may have been terminated from his or her present employment. The victim should file a claim with the state's unemployment fund while he or she is unemployed.

Moreover, the injured victim of a criminal act while operating is or her auto, may file a claim with their insurance company according to the uninsured or underinsured provision of their policy.

Also, Congress passed federal laws that granted relief to victims of insurance "redlining"; which is an illegal discriminatory practice that results in the denial of coverage. The Department of Housing and Urban Development Act set up Fair Access to Insurance Requirements (FAIR) plans to make sure that property owners were not denied fire damage coverage solely because the neighborhood had a high rate of arson cases.[13]

SUMMARY

The insurance coverage can repay losses from assaults, car thefts, burglaries, and robberies. However, the use of insurance to offset the effects of crime has several shortcomings. Foremost, among these is the fact that citizens must purchase insurance. The fact that many people cannot afford insurance premiums effectively places insurance beyond their reach. Many ague that insurance is a means of offsetting crime losses actually penalizes the victim further by assuming that it is the victim's responsibility to take action and avoid crime. Another problem is that most insurance policies have a deductible amount clause that reduces the cash outlay to victims. Deductibles of $200 or $500 effectively eliminate any insurance payments for many crimes. In general, while insurance is a possible method for recouping losses, it is not an effective means in many instances.

CHAPTER ASSIGNMENT

You must contact an insurance company and complete the checklist as far as the establishment of a victim-assistance provision of an insurance claim.

VICTIM ASSISTANCE INSURANCE POLICY

1. Deductibles: (a)$100, (b)$200, $300, (c)$400, $500, $600
   Explain the ------------ for the deductible selected:_____
   _____
   _____
   _____
   _____

2. Medical Coverage:_____
   _____
   _____
   _____
   _____

3. Personal Property Losses:_____
   _____
   _____
   _____
   _____

4. Vandalism:_____
   _____
   _____
   _____
   _____

5. Loss of Income:_____
   _____
   _____
   _____
   _____

6. Death Benefits:_____
   _____
   _____
   _____
   _____

7. Disability Coverage:_____
   _____
   _____
   _____

CHAPTER EIGHT

VICTIM COMPENSATION PROGRAMS

INTRODUCTION

Victim compensation takes place when the state rather than the perpetrator, reimburses the victim for losses sustained at the hands of the offender or criminal. It has been stated that some victim compensation operations derive money from offender restitution, the state is the entity that has direct contact with the victim. Victim compensation is not a new concept. These remedies once existed thousands of years ago.

DEFINITION OF CONCEPTS

1. Victim Compensation: The reimbursement of the victim's losses due to a criminal act by the state.
2. Babylonian Code of Hummurabi: The earliest reference to governmental compensation for crime victims.
3. Margery Fry: An English Magistrate who sparked the interest to revive compensation in the late 1950s.
4. Benefit Criteria: Cover primary costs – medical to funeral expenses.
5. Replacement Services: Funds for works, childcare and housekeeping the victim.
6. Forfeiture of Assets Laws: Prevents vicious offenders from being showered with lucrative offers of book contracts and other money generating royalties.
7. Son of Sam Laws: Laws that prevented financial exploitation of crime by their perpetrators.
8. Notoriety for Profit Laws: Symbolic gestures that inform perpetrators that crime doesn't pay and they must hand over the money they received to the innocent victims.14

HISTORICAL DEVELOPMENT

The earliest reference to governmental compensation for crime victims can be traced to the ancient Babylonian Code of Hummurabi (about 1775 B.C.), which is considered to be the oldest written body of criminal law. The Code instructed territorial governors to replace a robbery victim's lost property if the criminal was not captured; in the case of a murder, the governor was to pay the heirs a specific sum in silver from the treasury. In the centuries that followed, restitution by the offender replaced compensation by the state. During the Middle Ages, restitution faded away and victims had no avenue to redress except to try to recover losses by suing in civil court.15

The interest in compensation revived during the 1980's, when the prison reform movement in Europe focused its attention on the suffering of convicts and in doing so indirectly called attention to the plight of their victims.

Legal historians have uncovered only a few scattered instances of special funds that were set aside for crime victims: one is Tuscany, another in Mexico and one in France, Switzerland, and Cuba also experimented with the victim compensation programs.

An English Magistrate, Margery Fry has been widely acknowledged as the prison reformer who sparked the revival of interest in compensation in Anglo-Saxon legal system in the late 1950's. Because of her efforts a government commission investigated different reparations proposals and set up a fund in 1964 in Great Britain. Several Australian states and Canadian provinces followed suit during the next few years.

In the latter part of 1950's, the question of compensation surfaced in America law journals. Initially, distinguished scholars raised many objections to the idea of government aid to crime victims. But support for the notion of compensation grew when a U.S. Supreme Court Justice, Arthur Goldberg alleged that society should assume some responsibility for making whole again those whom the laws had failed to protect.

In 1965, California became the first state to initiate a repayment process as part of its public assistance system. Subsequently, New York created a special board to allocate reimbursements to crime victims. However, 50 states enacted legislation to compensated victims of crime for their losses.

OBJECTIVES

The victim compensation programs will focus on the following objectives that are the basic principles of policy development:

1. Victim compensation programs should establish goals to adequately process claims as in a expeditious manner.
2. States should examine the nature, level and scope of benefits.
3. Victim compensations should expand the types of victims eligible to receive counseling benefits.
4. Victim compensation programs should increase medical benefits for victims of catastrophic physical injury.
5. Victim compensation programs should eliminate restitution requirements and permit victims to report the crime within a reasonable period of time.
6. Victim compensation programs should coordinate with victim assistance programs to develop an effective community outreach strategy.
7. Victim compensation programs have a duty to listen to and address the issues of the victim.
8. To ensure programs that victim advocates and allied professionals are fully informed of the scope of compensation.
9. Should make effective use of advanced technological – automated claims and electronic linkage with medical providers and etc.
10. State compensation should work with other state programs that provide funding for victim services.

ELIGIBILITY REQUIREMENTS FOR VICTIMS

Each state had eligibility requirements victims must meet to qualify for compensation benefits. While eligibility requirements vary from state to state, virtually all programs require victims to:

1. Report the crime promptly to law enforcement. Seventy-two hours is the general standard. Most states have good cause exceptions that apply liberally to children, incapacitated victims and others with special circumstances.
2. Cooperate with police and prosecutors in the investigation and prosecution of the case.
3. Submit a timely application to the compensation program, generally within one year from the date of the crime. The children are exempted from the timely filing requirements.

Victims are required to provide other essential information as needed by the program and they are not eligible for compensation if the victimization given rises to the claim resulted from the claimant's own criminal activity or significant misconduct.

BENEFIT CRITERIA

All compensation programs cover the same major types of expenses, although their specific limits vary. The primary costs covered by all states are:

1. Medical expenses
2. Mental Health counseling
3. Lost of wages for victims unable to work
4. Lost support for dependents of homicide victims
5. Funeral expenses

In addition, many programs pay for other essential expenses resulting form violent crime. They include:

1. Moving or relocation expenses
2. Transportation to medical providers
3. Replacement services for work such as child care and housekeeping the victim
4. Essential personal possessions lost or damaged during the crime, such as eye glasses or hearing aids
5. Crime-scene clean up
6. Rehabilitation, which may include physical or job therapy, ramps, wheelchairs and modification of homes or vehicles

CRIME VICTIMS

Victims who have suffered physical injury or extreme mental distress as a result of one or more of the following crimes:

1. Aggravated Assault
2. Aggravated Battery
3. Criminal Sexual Contact of a minor
4. Criminal Sexual Penetration
5. Murder
6. Voluntary Manslaughter
7. Involuntary Manslaughter
8. Abandonment or Abuse of a child
9. Homicide by vehicle
10. Stalking
11. Kidnapping
12. Arson resulting in bodily injury
13. Aggravated Arson
14. Aggravated Indecent Exposure
15. Dangerous use of explosives or
16. Negligent use of a deadly weapon

EXTRAPOLATING PROFITS

The victim may pursue and additional option for recovering losses or their survivors: going after the profits made by offenders who sell their first hand accounts of how and why they committed their crimes. In a few cases each year, offenders cash in on the sensationalism surrounding their highly publicized crimes. The question that arises is whether victims can take these fruits of crime away from offenders.

Some states passed forfeiture of assets laws to prevent a vicious serial killer from being showered with lucrative offers for:

1. Book Contracts
2. Movie Rights
3. Paid Appearances to disclose the story about the crime

Subsequently, all states and the federal government enacted similar laws called "Son of Sam laws" to prevent financial exploitation of crimes by their perpetrators. These statutes went after financial gains in the form of fees, advances, and royalties from any reenactments of the heinous deeds in movies, memories, books, magazine articles, tape recordings, phonograph records, radio programs, television shows or other forms of entertainment.

The Notoriety for Profit laws were primarily symbolic gestures to drive home the message that crime doesn't pay, but they also were intended to expedite the handling over the money to innocent victims.

SUMMARY

Victim compensation funds have been set up in most states since the early 1960's although they initially met considerable political resistance. To obtain reimbursements, it is not necessary that the offender be apprehended and convicted. However, only innocent victims of violent crimes, not property related crimes are eligible for financial aid to cover lost earnings and out of pocket medical expenses. Many state funds do not have enough money from penalty assessments and the general treasury to quickly and adequately reimburse violent crime victims.

A small number of victims might be able to pursue their claims by attaching a portion of the money certain convicts make by cashing in on their notoriety.

CHAPTER ASSIGNMENT

Most state victim compensation programs produce an annual report that details such information as the number of claims filed, number of awards and denials, amount of monies awarded and other details. Obtain the annual reports of two neighboring state's victim compensation programs and design a parallel comparison of the two and complete the following.

PARALLEL COMPARISON OF
TWO STATES VICTIM COMPENSATION ANNUAL REPORTS

State of _____   State of _____
1. Number of Claims Filed_____   1. Number of Claims Filed_____
2. Number of Awards_____   2. Number of Awards_____
3. Number of Denials_____   3. Number of Denials_____
4. Amount of Monies Awarded_____   4. Amount of Monies Awarded_____
5. Emergency Monies Awarded_____   5. Emergency Monies Awarded_____

What did you find when you compared and contrasted the two state programs?_____

_____

_____

_____

_____

_____

_____

OVC NATIONAL DIRECTORY OF
VICTIM ASSISTANCE FUNDING OPPORTUNITIES 2001

STATE	ADMINISTRATOR(S)	PHONE NUMBER	FAX NUMBER
Alabama	Martin Ramsay mramsay@acvcc.state.at.us	(334) 242-4007	(334) 353-1401
Alaska	Susan Browne Susan_browne@dps.state.ak.us	(800) 764-3040	(907) 465-2379
Arizona	Donna Marcum dmarcum@acjc.state.az.us	(602) 230-0252x208	(602) 728-0752
Arkansas	Kathy Sheehan kathys@ag.state.ar.us	(501) 682-3656	(501) 682-5313
California	Skip Ellsworth sellsworth@boc.ca.gov	(916) 327-0394	(916) 327-2933
Colorado	Deborah Kasyon Deborah.kasyon@edps.state.co.us	(303) 239-4402	(303) 239-4411
Connecticut	Linda Cimino Linda.cimino@jud.state.ct.us	(860) 747-6070	(860) 747-6428
Delaware	Joseph Hughes	(302) 995-8383	(302) 995-8387
District of Columbia	Laura Banks Reed reedlb@dcsc.gov	(202) 879-4216	(202) 879-4230
Florida	Gwen Roache Gwen_roache@org.state.fl.us	(904) 414-3300	(904) 487-1595
Georgia	Shawanda Reynolds-Cobb sreynold@cjcc.state.ga.us	(404) 559-4949	(404) 559-4960
Hawaii	Pamela Serguson-Brey Psserguson-brey.@lava.net	(808) 587-1143	(808) 587-1146
Idaho	George Gutierrez ggutierr@iic.state.id.us	(208) 334-6070	(208) 334-5145
Illinois	Martha Newton mnewton@atg.state.il.us	(312) 814-2581	(312) 814-5079
Indiana	Gregory Hege ghege@cji.state.in.us	(317) 233-3383	(317) 232-4979
Iowa	Julie Swanston jswanst@ag.state.ia.us	(515) 281-5044	(515) 281-8199
Kansas	Frank Henderson, Jr. hendersf@at02po.wpo.state.ks.us	(785) 296-2359	(785) 296-0652
Kentucky	Sheila Tharpe Sheila.tharpe@mail.state.ky.us	(502) 564-7986	(502) 564-4817
Louisiana	Bob Wertz bobw@cole.state.la.us	(225) 925-4437	(225) 925-1998
Maine	Deborah Shaw Rice Deb.rice@state.me.us	(207) 626-8589	(207) 624-7730

Maryland	Robin Woolford, Jr. rwoolford@dpscs.state.mn.us	(410) 585-3042	(410) 764-4373
Massachusetts	Cheryl Watson Cheryl.Watson@ago.state.ma.us	(617) 727-2200	(617) 367-3906
Michigan	Michael Fullwood fullwoodm@state.mi.us	(517) 373-0979	(517) 241-2769
Minnesota	Marie Bibus Marie.bibus@state.mn.us	(651) 282-6267	(612) 296-5787
Mississippi	Sandra Morrison morriss@dfa.state.ms.us	(601) 359-6766	(601) 359-3262
Missouri	Susan Sudduth ssudduth@central.dolir.state.mo.us	(573) 526-3511	(573) 526-4940
Montana	Kathy Matson kmatson@state.mt.us	(406) 444-3653	(406) 444-4722
Nebraska	Nancy Steeves nsteeves@crimecome.state.ne.us	(402) 471-2194	(402) 471-2837
Nevada	Patricia Moore	(702) 486-2740	(702) 486-2555
New Hampshire	Kim Therrien ktherrien@doj.state.nh.us	(603) 271-1284	(603) 271-2110
New Jersey	Jim Casserly Jamescasserly@excite.com	(973) 648-2107x7716	(973) 648-7031
New Mexico	Larry Tackman Larry.tackman@state.mn.us	(505) 841-9432	(505) 841-9437
New York	Jennifer Pirrone jpirrone@nysnet.net	(518) 457-8003	(518) 457-8658
North Carolina	Robert Reives rreives@nccrimecontrol.org	(919) 733-7974	(919) 715-4209
North Dakota	Paul Coughlin Pcoughli@state.nd.us	(701) 328-6195	(701) 328-6651
Ohio	Brian Cook bcook@ag.state.oh.us	(614) 466-5610	(614) 752-2732
Oklahoma	Suzanne Breedlove breedlos@dac.state.ok.us	(405) 264-5006	(405) 264-5097
Oregon	Connie Gallagher	(503) 378-5348	(503) 378-5738
Pennsylvania	Carol Lavery lavery@pccd.state.pa.us	(717) 783-0551x3215	(717) 783-7713
Puerto Rico	Lidice Candelario	(787) 724-0435	(787) 724-0928
Rhode Island	Catherine King Avila cavila@treasury.state.ri.us	(401) 277-2287	(401) 222-2212
South Carolina	Renee Graham rgraham@govepp.state.sc.us	(803) 734-1930	(803) 734-1708
South Dakota	Ann Holzhauser Ann.holzhauser@state.sd.us	(605) 773-6317	(605) 773-6834

Tennessee	Amy Dunlap adunlap@mail.state.tn.us	(615) 741-2734	(615) 532-4979
Texas	Rex Uberman Rex.uberman@oag.state.tx.us	(512) 936-1200	(512) 320-8270
Utah	Dan R. Davis ddavis@gov.state.ut.us	(801) 238-2360	(801) 533-4127
Vermont	Lori Hayes lhayes@ccvs.state.vt.us	(802) 241-1250	(802) 241-1253
Virginia	William Dudley William.Dudley@vwc.state.va.us	(804) 378-4371	(804) 367-9740
Washington	Cletus Nnanabu Nnan235@lni.wa.gov	(360) 902-5340	(360) 902-5333
West Virginia	John Fulks jferderspiel@wvdcjs.org	(304) 347-4851	(304) 347-4915
Wisconsin	Gretchen MacDonald macdonaldsgi@doj.state.wi.us	(608) 266-6470	(608) 264-6368
Wyoming	Sharon Montagnino smonta@missc.state.wy.us	(307) 777-7200	(307) 777-6683

CHAPTER NINE

VICTIMS OF MURDER

INTRODUCTION

The United States differs very much from other countries due to the amount of criminal violence continues to increase the death toll. Murder is a common denominator in the urban areas, but the surrounding jurisdictions have been noting a substantial step-up of deaths.

This chapter will examine the dynamics that underlie criminal violence. Most killers murder someone they know rather than killing a complete stranger. No one deserves to be murdered and not because they are elderly or infirm, or exhibit behavior others don't disagree with or they have vital differences.

A single murder can tear at the fibers of an entire community, or even leave scars on a nation. Murder can bring ordinary persons into the involvement with the medical examiner, law enforcement, the district attorney or the prosecutor, the judicial system and even the media. To investigate and try one case can cost hundreds of thousands of dollars. And if the killer is not apprehended and brought to justice, clouds of suspicion can linger and other citizens may even be endangered.

Worst of all, are the psychological wounds on the survivors - wounds as deep and serious as those that killed their loved ones. These wounds are not always obvious, but they cannot be ignored, or they, like physical wounds, will fester and grow even more worse.

Finally, no treatment of murder would be complete without examining at the silent or hidden sufferers of murder: the survivors of the deceased. In their context, we will examine the death notification process and the bereavement process endured by the victim's relative.

OBJECTIVES

The students will be able to ascertain the vital concepts of this chapter and the learning objectives will articulate the following:

1. Define criminal homicide
2. Define a mushroom shooting
3. Discuss the regional culture of violence thesis
4. Introduce the term 'trauma' and explain its relevance
5. Relay the details of the death notification process
6. Discuss the grief process and its different stages
7. Explain some of the adjustments faced by the survivors of homicide
8. List the various survivors patterns and how they differ in response to the homicide event

DEFINITION OF CONCEPTS

1. Criminal Homicide: The willful non-negligent) killing of one human being by another.
2. Mushroom Shooting: Stray bullets that are not intended for any one particular person.
3. Regional Culture of Violence Thesis: Southern individuals were responsible for the differential distribution of homicide victimization rates throughout the U.S..
4. Trauma: Refers to any physical injury without any concern for the origin of the damages.
5. Autopsy Method: Postmortem reviews of the deceased.
6. Death Notification: Informing the next-of-kin or other survivors of the deceased.
7. Bereavement Process: The lost of a love one or next-of-kin involves four stages:
   a. Shock and denial,
   b. Anger,
   c. Isolation,
   d. Acceptance and Recovery
8. Domestic Violence Homicide Survival Patterns: The survivor may feel some personal guilt for failing to intervene.
9. Gang-Related Homicide Survival Pattern: The survivors feel he or she had no control over the event.
10. Golden Hour: The time period in which serious injured people need medical attention if they are survive.[16]

THE BEREAVEMENT PROCESS

The death of a significant other, particularly through homicide is a sudden, emotionally shattering event that can quickly propel survivors deep into a crisis state.

Survivors do not have the luxury of anticipatory grief which the preparations that people can make to cushion the impact of death when a loss is imminent or expected to take place. For example you can make preparations for a terminable ill love one or relative, but a sudden loss of another is difficult for the survivor to adapt expeditiously to the loss. Homicide survivors lack this preparation.

Most homicide victims are men under the age of 40. The impact of the family is immediate and it becomes very difficult for the family to cope without the loss of the father. Their children will grow up without them. The widows must assume all family responsibilities and most important the financial demands become a heavy burden. The social security and insurance may help defer some expenses but the family unit is altered due to the loss of the father.

Some women may find that they must reenter the job market or seek additional employment (part-time) to sustain the family finances.

The grief process entails four stages:

1. Shock and Denial: Immediately after being informed of the death, the survivor reacts in denying the information.
2. Anger: The survivors tend to vent his or her rage, frustration, and anger toward anyone or anything they encounter.
3. Isolation: The survivor will isolate himself or herself from others. Isolation reflects different emotions ranging from uncertainty with no one to aid them.
4. Acceptance and Recovery: The survivor begins to resume some form of normal activities in the acceptance and recovery stage. The death remains with the individual, but the event is incorporated into the daily routine as he or she realizes that life must exist.

The key to the bereavement process is the provision of support to the survivor. The support may commence with the police officer or the physician who notifies the survivor, and may last over a long period of time. In some communities, we are seeing the homicide support groups whom they serve or assist the survivor for a short or long term.[17]

SUMMARY

The murder is a deliberate killing of one human being by another with malice forethought. Murder has reached epidemic levels and it is considered to be a leading cause of death among various ethnic groups within the United States of America. The spreading of violence appears that the bloodshed will not slow down any time soon.

It is the murder survivors - the young children who's will carry the worst emotional scars. They are forced to reclaim their shattered lives and make some sense out of the aftermath of the murder.

CHAPTER ASSIGNMENT

Define the following concepts as it relates to murder:

1. Intimate Femicide: _____

_____

_____

2. Felony Murder: _____

_____

_____

3. Parricide: _____

_____

_____

4. Patricide: _____

_____

_____

5. Matricide: _____

_____

_____

6. Trauma: _____

_____

_____

7. Mushroom Shooting: _____

_____

_____

8. Firearm Fatality Reporting System: _____

_____

_____

9. Golden Hour: _____

_____

_____

10. Autopsy Method: _____

_____

_____

CHAPTER TEN

KIDNAPPING AND ABDUCTIONS OF CHILDREN

INTRODUCTION

Taking and holding a person against his or her will for some nefarious purpose was recognized many years ago as a vicious act under the English common law. Today, in state and federal statutes, force is not a necessary element of the crime.

The victim can be detained through tricking or manipulation (what is called inveiglement). Besides extorting a ransom, the kidnapper or abductor may intend to rob the captive (for example, compel an adult to withdraw money from an automated teller machine, exploit the person as a mere sex object, keep and raise a very young child, or cruelly snuff out a life. If the kidnapper makes a ransom demand or transports the hostage across state lines, then the federal statures are violated and the FBI can enter the manhunt.

KIDNAPPING

The maximalists alarmist are individuals argue that an over looked problem is reaching epidemic proportions. Dire consequences will follow unless drastic steps are taken. The maximalists believe or assume the worst can happen. Also, the maximalists believed that kidnapping had become frighteningly common and that a complacent public need to become aroused and mobilized. They warned that child snatchers were everywhere, no youngster was ever completely safe, and parents could never be too careful about taking precautions and restricting their children's activities.

There are 200 to 300 kidnappings of children by adult per year. The abductor intends to permanently keep the child, extort a ransom, or commit some other crime, including murder. In most of these extremely serious offenses, the kidnapper is not a complete stranger, but instead is a disgruntled former boyfriend or the child's mother or a friend of the family.

SHORT-TERM ABDUCTIONS

There are between 3200 to 4600 short-term abductions by non-family member per year. These cases most of all the legal elements of the kidnapping: a crime by an acquaintance or by a complete stranger who takes the child by force or by deceit into a building, vehicle, or some other place, and, or detains the child for more than an hour.

A substantial number of abductions committed by strangers were reported by caretakers of the children.

LONG-TERM ABDUCTIONS

There were approximately 163,000 abductions committed by a family member per year. In these cases, a family member is usually a parent that takes a child in violation of a family court decree and tries to conceal the taking of the child and moves the child to another state permanently, or alters the custodial arrangements.

These abductions were most likely to occur during January and August, when school vacations and parental visits end.

THE REDUCTION OF PARENTAL ABDUCTION RISKS

There is no amount of precaution can completely protect you from a spouse or ex-spouse who intends in taking the children. You can take some steps to reduce the risks:

1. Obtain legal, permanent or temporary custody of your child. If no legal custody has been obtained, the abducting spouse has but violated any laws.
2. Once you have obtained legal custody, secure a passport for your children and notify the passport office that your children are not to be taken out of the country without your written permission.
3. If the spouse or ex-spouse is threatening to abduct, have the threats witnessed or tape-recorded with discretion.
   a. The parent who is seeking visitation the parent can be ordered to post a sizable bond. If he or she leaves, then the money goes to you.
   b. Make sure that your custody order details police procedure. If the order is violated, the police have specific authorization by the court to retrieve the child if necessary.
   c. Place restrictions upon where visitations may take place.
4. Know and maintain current vital information about your spouse or ex-spouse, such as social security, driver's license number, license plate number, and credit information.
5. Don't frustrate or manipulate the ex-spouse's visitation time if he or she is behaving responsibly in accordance with the custody agreement. The frustration and anger can cause the parent to contemplate snatching the children.
6. Attempt to maintain a friendly, or at least civil relationship with your spouse or ex-spouse for the well being of the children.
7. If your child is school age or attends a day care center, or stays with a babysitter, submit a certified copy of the custody order with a photo of the other parent.
8. Talk with your children, and teach them what to do in case of an abduction. Tell them that you will always want them and that you are alive and you are searching for them.18

STRANGER ABDUCTIONS - REDUCING THE RISKS

The abduction of your child by a stranger is every parent's nightmare. Fortunately, there are precautions you can teach your child to help reduce the risks of being abducted.

1. Never leave the child unattended in a car, supermarket, or shopping center, or at home alone.

2. Instruct your child not to go with any stranger.
3. Don't purchase or dress your child in a T-shirt with his or her name printed on it. Knowing a child's name is a first step to familiarity.
4. Teach your children that a stranger is also somebody they don't know.
5. Encourage children to have buddies. Children like to do things in pairs.
6. Have the children to do a project in which they write their entire name, address, and telephone number with area code.
7. Show your children how to use a telephone, explain what an area code means and what it does.
8. Tell the children that most adults will help them rather then hurt them.
9. Teach your children to be alert. If someone is hanging around, or driving around in a car, take a good look at the person's face and car.[19]

SUMMARY

Many groups of victims face special problems that require special solutions. The distraught parents of missing children need to convince authorities that their youngsters were truly victims of foul play and to take immediate action. There are numerous child-search organizations that are operated by volunteers that can help to mobilize manhunts, and state-clearing houses for information about missing children can coordinate activities.

Most states now require police officers to take on how to investigate missing children cases, to interact with their families and to follow the FBI's Child Abduction Response Plan.

CHAPTER ASSIGNMENT

You must obtain a copy of your state's kidnapping or abduction statute. Does your state law cover the following:

1. Short-term Abduction: _____

\
_____

_____

_____

_____

_____

2. Long-term Abduction: _____

\
_____

_____

_____

_____

Also, list at least six ways that you reduce parental abduction risks:

_____

_____

_____

_____

_____

_____

CHAPTER ELEVEN

VICTIMS OF CHILD ABUSE

INTRODUCTION

Children are more vulnerable to victimization because of their age, size, and dependence on adults. Children have little or no control over the lives in their home or who associates with members of the household. There are certain children who are targeted more frequently; including the shy, lonely, and compliant children, as well as pre-verbal and very young children those kids are labeled as "bad kids". Children with physical, emotional or developmental disabilities are particularly vulnerable to victimization.

OBJECTIVES

The student will be able to ascertain the subsequent after reading this chapter:

1. Explain the difference between abuse and neglect
2. Understand what the term maltreatment includes
3. Recognize symptoms of sexual abuse
4. Explain how maltreatment can take the form of emotional abuse
5. List the items that should be included in a maltreatment report
6. Gain an understanding of the concepts incidence and prevalence.

DEFINITION OF CONCEPTS

1. Maltreatment: Acts of omission as well as commission, including, neglect, physical abuse, sexual abuse and emotional abuse.
2. Neglect: The range of abandonment to the failure to meet a child's 3 basic requirements:
   a. Physical – basic supervision
   b. Emotional – nurturing and affection
   c. Educational – providing support for academic or educational learning
3. Physical Abuse: Involved assaults – punching, kicking, scalding, suffocating, shaking and extended confinement and excessive punishments.
4. Sexual Abuse: Are recognized as incest, fondling, sodomy, intercourse, rape, and impairment of the child's morals.
5. Emotional Abuse: Serious or mental disorder.
6. Prevalence: Proportion of people in some population being studied who have ever suffered this form of victimization.
7. Incidence: New cases that come to light each year.
8. Pedophiles: Child molesters.[20]

SIGNS AND SYMPTOMS OF CHILD ABUSE

Some signs and symptoms of child abuse include:

1. Head injury and/or multiple injuries to the body.
2. Frequent bacterial infection, genital rash, and vaginal discharge.
3. Fractures or bruises in an infant who has not started to learn how to walk.
4. Immersion burns from scalding hot water and cigarette burns.
5. Injury to buttocks or scalp (bruising or hair loss).
6. Injury to thin body parts (chins, knee, elbows, and etc.).
7. Dramatic academic changes, disruptive or overly aggressive behavior.
8. Emotional/behavioral changes, runaway, truancy, and drug abuse.
9. Interest in sexual acts or display of sexual knowledge beyond the child's years.
10. Masturbatory behavior.
11. Extremely passive.
12. Withdrawn or hostile towards authority figures.

PREVENTION STRATEGIES

What can be done to ensure that all children have a safe home and a loving atmosphere in which to grow and develop.

The Parents Anonymous is a nonprofit organization that local chapters throughout the United States. They offer a unique and effective approach to strengthening families based upon the subsequent principles and its importance:

1. Mutual Assistance: The parents take the lead in achieving personal and family growth. Parents are responsible for their own growth, as well as for reaching out to others.
2. Empowerment: Parents have the ability to take charge of their lives by seeking solutions for their problems.
3. Support: Mutual learning and individual growth is achieved by providing a non-threatening environment.
4. Ownership: The group belongs to its members and they control the content of the weekly meetings.
5. Caring: Group members create an atmosphere of belonging and acceptance in which healthy-family interacts.
6. Non-violence: No violence is permitted among family members.
7. Anonymity and Confidentiality: Parents have the right to withhold their names from others.[21]

COUNSELING

Another avenue for dealing with child abuse cases emphasizes a treatment or rehabilitation approach. This response seeks to help both the victim and the offender, often involving the entire family. Most treatment interventions resolve around individual and group counseling. The counseling help to open-up the lines of communication. The communication helps the individuals to cope with their problems.

EDUCATION

The education efforts aim to demystify child rearing by providing parents with instruction in child development. Many advocate the continuing of adult education projects at hospitals, schools, churches, and social service agencies. Moreover, once this approach is in place, it would require several years before yielding positive dividends.

SUMMARY

It has taken our society a great deal of time to recognize that child abuse exists. The state has enacted legislation forbidding the victimization of children. Child abuse tends to take place behind closed doors. It often involve victim who are unable to defend themselves, making detection difficult.

There are numerous coping strategies, however, they suggest that the eradication of child abuse and neglect is everybody's responsibility. Finally, somewhere in this country, another child died from abuse or neglect in time it took to read this chapter.

CHAPTER ASSIGNMENT

You are required to read your state's child abuse and neglect laws. Also, you must list at least ten individuals that would be an asset to an Advisory Board of Child Abuse and Neglected Children:

1. _____

2. _____

3. _____

4. _____

5. _____

6. _____

7. _____

8. _____

9. _____

10. _____

Provide a reason for the selection of each individual.

CHAPTER TWELVE

VICTIMS OF ELDER ABUSE

INTRODUCTION

Who are the elderly? Rather than lumping everybody into a certain single age category, there are numerous groupings that have been presented. An examination of the crime statistics reveals that the elderly have the lowest odds of becoming crime victims. The average life expectancy has risen considerably which translates into older persons comprising a sizable segment of the population.

However, the entire population is becoming "grayer". The population data is showing that the baby boomers are now moving into their midlife. The elderly constitute a substantial amount of the very active political constituency. Moreover, they vote, lobby, and they participate in the legislative process.

Despite greatly reduced chances of victimization, the elderly are extremely fearful of falling prey to criminals.

A growing social problem that has gained recognition in recent years is elder abuse and neglect. Caretakers maltreat the elderly. Economic pressure, role reversals and other tensions sometimes make it difficult to provide appropriate extended care.

OBJECTIVES

The students will ascertain the following objectives upon reading of the chapter:

1. Explain who the elderly are
2. Discuss the objective odds of elder victimization
3. Talk about age patterns in victimization statistics
4. Demonstrate the "graying" of American population
5. List risk factors of the elderly
6. Recognize symptoms of elderly abuse
7. How to spot warning signs of financial abuse of the elderly
8. How to prevent and respond to elder abuse, neglect, exploitation and other crimes

DEFINITION OF CONCEPTS

1. Elder Abuse: It's the mistreatment or neglect of an older person, usually by a relative or other caregiver.
2. Physical Abuse: Victims are kicked, punched, beaten, and even raped. Pain, injury or death may result.
3. Neglect: Failure to provide medicine, food, or personal care.
4. Financial Exploitation: Abusers may steal or mismanage money, property, savings or credit cards.
5. Psychological Abuse: Older people may be intentionally isolated or derived companionship.
6. Other Abuse:

a. Older people may be forced to live in unsanitary conditions, or in poorly heated or cooled rooms.
b. Over medicating or withholding aids, eyeglasses, and dentures.

WHO ARE THE VICTIMS OF ELDER ABUSE?

The victims often live with family members and depend on them for daily care. The victims are more likely to be:

1. Age 75 or over
2. Women
3. Dependent on the abuser for basic needs
4. Suffering from a mental or physical illness

WHO ARE THE ABUSERS?

They're family members who are acting as caregivers. Abusers often suffer from:

1. Stress
2. Alcohol and other drug problems
3. Dependency: The abuser may depend on the older person for basic needs or housing and money.

WHY DOES ELDER ABUSE HAPPEN?

The experts believe many factors may be involved:

1. Resentment: Caring for an elderly parent can be exhausting and resentment can build, which may lead to abuse.
2. Life Crises: Living with the elderly parent can cause severe stress, especially of family members who are struggling with personal problems.
3. Lack of Love and Friendship: Often, a dependent parent returns to his or her family after being away for many years.
4. Attitudes Toward Violence: Violence is seen as an acceptable way to solve problems.
5. Retaliation: Some abusers may try to get back at their parents for post mistreatment.
6. Lack of Services: Without needed health and social services in the community, caregivers may be unable to handle the responsibility of caring for an elderly parent.
7. Money Problems: Many families are on limited or fixed incomes. The relative or caregiver may be depended on the older person for money.
8. Social Problems: Unemployment, poor or crowded housing or other living conditions may contribute to elder abuse.

WHY DOES THE PROBLEM CONTINUE?

The following represent the possible reasons:

1. Denial: Some older people simply refuse to accept the fact that they are being abused by their loved ones.
2. Physical/Mental Illness: Older people must overcome the obstacles.
3. Lack of Services: Temporary shelters and facilities are lacking for older persons.
4. Fear and Shame: Older people are afraid of retaliation or too ashamed to take action.
5. Lack of Involvement: Friends, relatives, or neighbors may tolerate abuse because they believe families should handle their own problems.
6. Dependence: Many feel that they have no one to turn to for help.
7. Lack of Awareness: They may not be aware of the professional agencies available to help them.
8. Isolation: No contact with others outside the home.

PREVENTION

Everyone can help stop elder abuse. The society can help by supporting the following:

1. Prevention Programs: Usually state agencies have Elderly or Senior Citizen Protective Service Programs.
2. Education: To fight negative attitudes toward older persons and people who have disabilities.
3. Resources:
   a. Home Health Aids
   b. Meal Delivery
   c. Day Care
   d. Transportation
   e. Counseling
   f. Assisted Living [22]

SUMMARY

The elder abuse poses a relatively new problem for the criminal justice system. While abuse may not be a new problem occurrence, it is a phenomenon that is just now gaining attention. Victimologists are beginning to identify the intricacies of the problem, probe its causes and offer some solutions. However, a great deal of additional work remains to be done at both the theoretical and practical levels.

As time marches on, we must develop more ways to detect and prevent the new symptoms and signs of the elder abuse.

CHAPTER ASSIGNMENT

You must visit a nursing home and interview an elderly person and develop an elderly abuse list sheet:

ELDER ABUSE LIST

1. _____

2. _____

3. _____

4. _____

5. _____

6. _____

7. _____

8. _____

9. _____

10. _____

CHAPTER THIRTEEN

VICTIMS OF SPOUSE ABUSE

INTRODUCTION

Every day thousands of husbands inflict injuries on their wives. A substantial amount of the violence is hidden from the public. It will frequently take place within their privacy but no one can see the physical infliction or hear the anguished and frustrated pleas for help. Furthermore, the harsh and brutal sound of the beatings without any intervention.

It is only recently that we have come to realize the amount of human suffering that takes place within families. Finally, society has commenced to recognize the problem of family violence as a serious health hazard.

This chapter will articulate the violence found between husbands and wives, or other conjugal cohabitants. The historical domination of men over women forms of the cornerstone for this chapter.

OBJECTIVES

The student should be able to understand the following objectives after reading this chapter:

1. Estimate the extent of spouse abuse
2. Distinguish spouse abuse from domestic violence
3. Understand what the battered women syndrome means
4. Link masochism with spouse abuse
5. Articulate the cycle of violence theory

DEFINITION OF CONCEPTS

1. Intra-individual Theories: examine the cause of deviant behavior inside a person, or better known as psychopathological – stress, mental illness, depression, low self-esteem and other related problems.
2. Sociocultural Explanation (Patriarchy): women were the property of the father or husband and subject to control and discipline.
3. Social Learning Approach: learned helplessness: the woman cannot influence or control what is about to happen to them.
4. Battered-Women Syndrome: a self-defense argument, whereby the woman is so traumatized by previous beatings that she will seize the opportunity to kill their batterers to prevent further victimization episodes.

HISTORICAL DEVELOPMENT

The domination of men over women has strong historical roots. Early Roman law treated women as property of their husbands, a custom reinforced in Biblical passages, Christianity, English Common Law, and the customs of the American colonists.

Women have held no legal standing throughout most of history. Any harm committed against a women was viewed as an offense against the father or husband, not her. Subsequently, it was male owners who sought vengeance or compensation for his loss. At the same time, a female could not be considered to be the injured or aggrieved party. The father or husband was the one held responsible for any injurious action by his woman. However, the father or husbands were expected to punish women.

The move in this country to laws restricting wife beatings fit into three stages. The first occurred in the mid-1600's when the puritans enacted laws against wife beatings and family violence. However, these laws were rarely enforced.[23]

A second stage revealed that family violence appeared in the late 1800's, when states commenced enacting laws restricting family violence. Some states even required or mandated public flogging as a punishment for beating women. Once again, these laws were rarely enforced.

The third stage of intent in spousal violence is the one currently in effect. The call for law enforcement intervention into domestic violence replaced family privacy issues.

Perhaps the greatest impact upon spousal abuse was the publication in 1984 of the Minneapolis study of arresting abusive husbands.

THE CYCLE OF VIOLENCE THEORY

Contributions to this sense of helplessness is the reality that the battered women are not beaten every minute of the day. Instead there is a cycle of violence, which gradually builds the feelings of being powerless and unable to alter their plight. The cycle consist of three distinct stages:

1. The Tension-Builder Phase: There may be minor assaults, but the woman believes she can change her husbands' bullying behavior. She is willing to accept small isolated incidents.
2. The Battering Episode Phase: The men or husband is out of control and acts in a rage. A common rationalization to the volatile outbursts is the man's claim that he did not fully realize what he was doing because he had been drinking. This disinhibition account acts to transfer responsibility away from the abuser and to characterize alcohol as the real culprit.
3. The Reconciliation Phase: The husbands transform himself into a very apologetic, tender and loving character. The husband will give the wife a shower of affection and tokens of gifts.

SYMPTOMS AND SIGNS

1. Physical Abuse: abuse is usually recurrent and usually escalates both in frequency and severity. It may include the following:
   a. Pushing
   b. Shoving
   c. Slapping
   d. Hitting
   e. Kicking
   f. Holding and tying down or restraining the victim
   g. Inflicting bruises, lacerations, punctures, burns, scratches

2. Sexual Abuse: sexual abuse in violent relationships is often the most difficult aspect of abuse for women to discuss. It may include any form of forced sex or sexual degradation:

   a. Trying to make the victim perform sexual acts against her will
   b. Pursuing sexual activity when the victim is not fully conscious or is not asked or is afraid to say no
   c. Physically hurting the victim during sex or assaulting her genitals or the use of objects or weapons orally or anally

3. Psychological Abuse: psychological abuse may precede or accompany physical violence as means of controlling through fear and degradation. It may include the following:

   a. Threats of harm
   b. Physical and social isolation
   c. Extreme jealousy
   d. Intimidation
   e. Humiliation
   f. Constant criticizing
   g. Destroying the victim's trust 24

SUMMARY

Spouse abuse is gaining broad recognition as a pressing social problem. Individuals who profess to love one another hurt each other on a frequent or periodic bases. Abusive behavior appears to be almost an integral part of these marriages. It may be difficult for an outsider to comprehend why anyone would tolerate being victimized repeatedly in this way. However, as the learned helplessness perspective explains many women are trapped into staying in an abusive relationship. Fleeing from the abuser is not always a viable option.

The more prudent path for the criminal justice system to pursue in spouse abuse matters is to retain an open mind and be willing to try different approaches as research and practice dictate.

CHAPTER ASSIGNMENT

You are required to design a victim spousal abuse credit card. List the required information that must be introduced on the card.

1. _____

2. _____

3. _____

4. _____

5. _____

6. _____

7. _____

8. _____

9. _____

10. _____

11. _____

12. _____

Also, the credit card is approved by the family court for required necessities. You must list the subsequent necessities.

1. _____

2. _____

3. _____

4. _____

5. _____

6. _____

7. _____

8. _____

9. _____

10. _____

CHAPTER FOURTEEN

VICTIM ASSISTANCE - SEXUAL ASSAULTS

INTRODUCTION

Sexual assault is a devastating, and dehumanizing experience. What makes this crime so crushing is that it is a direct attack on the person's self. Many victims suffer tremendous feelings of humiliation and degradation because of their assailants. Many of these same emotions are rekindled when the victim turns to the criminal justice system expecting comfort and assistance.

This chapter will examine some of the theories that purport to explain why rape occurs. Many states have redrafted their laws in an effort to dismantle the traditional barriers to victim cooperation. For example, rape has become redefined as sexual assault.

Moreover, discussion of sexual assault will delve into the personal tragedy that victim experience, the healing process these people will face, and the common coping strategies.

OBJECTIVES

After reading this chapter, you should be able to:

1. Link a physiological explanation to rape behavior.
2. Relate the theme of male domination or power to rape.
3. Analyze the rape trauma syndrome.
4. Discuss what a crisis means?
5. Give the common law definition of rape.

DEFINITION OF CONCEPTS

1. Sexual Assault: Is the act of having non-consensual sex with another person.
2. Date Rape: Is when someone you are dating forces you to have sex.
3. Acquaintance Rape: Is when someone you know, but are not dating, forces you to have sex.
4. Date Rape Drugs: Is when someone gives you a drug, without your knowledge, with the intention of having sex with you.
5. Aggravated Sexual Assault: Is when a person knowingly causes another person to engage in a sexual act or attempts to do so by using force against that person, or by threatening or placing that person in fear who will be subjected to death, serious bodily injury or kidnapping.

HISTORICAL DEVELOPMENT

Rape or sexual assault is the most underreported crime in America. There have been significant changes to improve the treatment of sexual assault victims have occurred in the last two decades. The impact of reforms led by the woman's movement, can be seen in the legal, medical, mental health, and victim services arenas. During the 1970's the first rape crisis center was established.

EVOLUTION OF THE DEFINITION OF SEXUAL ASSAULT AND RAPE

Prior to the 1960's the legal definition of rape was generally a common law definition which was used throughout the United States and it was defined: rape as carnal knowledge of a woman not one's wife by force or against her will. In 1962, the definition was updated, defined rape as a man who has sexual intercourse with a female not his wife is guilty of rape, if he compels her to submit by force or threat or threat of imminent death or serious bodily injury.

However, most statutes retained a marital-rape exemption, and if focused on the victims consent rather than the perpetrator's forcible conduct.

In the 1970's and 1980's extensive rape reform laws were enacted throughout the United States and the legal definition of rape changed considerably. The states enacted rape statutes, which were called criminal sexual conduct, and sexual assault statutes. These statutes broaden the definition of rape and they possess the following characteristics:

1. Rape is defined as gender neutral, which broadens the earlier definition of rape to include men as well as women.
2. They include acts of sexual penetration other than vaginal penetration by a penis.
3. Threats as well as overt force are recognized as means to overpower the victim.

THE MEASUREMENT OF RAPE – SEXUAL ASSAULT

There is a major difference between rape cases and rape victims because women can be raped more than once. Also, there is a difference between the incidence of rape and the prevalence of rape. Incidence refers to the number of cases that occur in a given period of time, (usually a year), and incidence statistics are often reported as rates (the number of rapes per 100,000 women in the population). In contrast, prevalence, it refers to the percentage of women who have been raped in a specific period of time (within the past year or throughout their life time). Moreover, there is a difference between estimates based on reported versus non-reported rape cases. Finally, the estimates of rape are derived from two basic types of sources: official governmental sources and studies conducted by private researchers, which are often supported by grants from federal agencies. [25]

SEXUAL ASSAULTS

Sexual assault involves any act of sexual violence including date rape, spousal rape, stranger rape, unwanted touching, or any sexual behavior exhibited toward a child under the age of 15. There is a major misconception about sexual assault and most people believe these violent acts are carried out only by strangers. However, sexual assault is the fastest rising

96

violent crime in America today, stranger-rape is not the leading form of sexual assault. The majority of victims involved in non-fatal, violent sexual assault now, and more than likely trust the offender.

In many cases, the sexual offender and/or the victim had been drinking and/or using drugs. The use of alcohol or drugs is never an excuse to commit unwarranted sexual acts.

FACTS ABOUT DATE RAPE

Date rape is when someone you are dating forces you to have sex. However, examine the subsequent facts of date rape:

1. Date rape can happen on a first date or long into a relationship.
2. No matter who it is, if someone does not listen when you say no to sex, it is rape.
3. Rape is not about sex, it is about power and control.
4. Date rape often does not involve weapons or physical force: but rather threats to you or someone you care about if you refuse to have sex. This is considered to be rape.
5. You can always say no to having sex – even if you have been kissing or have had sex with that person in the past.
6. You can always change your mind about having sex. No matter what, NO means NO!
7. While there are others, alcohol is the original and most common date rape drug.
8. The highest number of rape victims are between the ages 11-17.
9. Nothing entitles someone to sex, not if they pay for your dinner, not if they buy you gifts, not if they become sexually aroused – Nothing.
10. Men are also victims of rape and sexual assault.

RAPE TRAUMA SYNDROME

The following are common responses to sexual assault and may be symptoms of the rape trauma syndrome.

1. Shock
2. Denial
3. Humiliation
4. Embarrassment
5. Self-blame
6. Guilt
7. Shame
8. Anger
9. Emotional Numbness
10. Nightmares
11. Phobias
12. Stomach Problems

13. Headaches

MYTHS ABOUT RAPE

MYTH #1: Rape is a street crime that only happens to women who put themselves in bad situations.
WRONG: Every eight minutes, someone is raped or assaulted, more often than not by someone they know and often in their own home. It can happen to you.

MYTH #2: Guys are sometimes oversexed and get carried away.
WRONG AGAIN: There is nothing romantic about sexual assault. Real love and intimacy are not expressed through force, power or humiliation. Rape is an act of hostile aggression, not uncontrollable passion.

MYTH #3: Girls who flirt or dress in sexy clothes are asking for it.
WRONG AGAIN: Like men, women have the right to dress as they please and flirting is an accepted part of most cultures.

PREVENTING DATE RAPE

There are various ways to reduce your chances of being sexually assaulted.

1. Know your date. Besides asking his name and address, get to know more about his ideas about women and relationships. If he is someone you do not know, arrange to meet in a public place.
2. Keep a clear head. Excessive use of alcohol or drugs can decrease your awareness and make you more vulnerable.
3. Be assertive. Do not be afraid to speak up if a situation makes you uncomfortable. Make it clear to your date that his paying for things doesn't give him rights to your body. It is always a good idea to have some money of your own with you.
4. Express yourself and expect to be respected. It may seem awkward at first, but tell your date how far you will go. It kissing is enough, say so, it can help avoid feelings of rejection or anger.
5. Trust your instincts. Do not deny danger signals around you. If someone displays a violent temper, tries to control you or will not take "no" for an answer, listen to what that behavior is telling you. Do not become a puppet.

RAPE PREVENTION
IN YOUR HOME

1. Make sure that your home has a door viewer and a deadbolt lock.
2. All entrances and garages should be well lighted.
3. Never hide a key over a door or in a flowerpot.

4. If single, don't put your first name on your mailbox or in the telephone book.
5. Do not admit strangers to your home under any circumstances.

RAPE PREVENTION
IN YOUR AUTOMOBILE

1. Always lock your car when leaving and entering it.
2. Always look in the back seat before entering the vehicle.
3. Have your keys in hand so you don't have to linger before entering.
4. If you have car trouble, raise the hood, lock yourself in, and wait for the police.
5. Do not stop to offer a ride to a stranded motorist: stop at the nearest phone booth and call the police.
6. If you suspect that someone is following you, drive to the nearest public place and blow your horn.

SEX OFFENDER NOTIFICATION
FOR NEIGHBORHOODS AND COMMUNITIES
(MEGANS LAW)

A sex offender is a person who has been convicted of a violation or attempted violation of any of the subsequent offenses, including, but not limited to:

1. Sexual abuse if the victim is under the age of 18.
2. Sexual conduct with a minor.
3. Sexual assault.
4. Molestation of a child.
5. Child prostitution.
6. Criminal sexual contact.

Prior to releasing the convicted sex offender from confinement, the Department of Corrections will notify the following:

1. County Sheriff
2. State Attorney General
3. County Prosecutor or District Attorney
4. Local Law Enforcement
5. County Probation Department
6. Division of Parole
7. Victims and Family
8. Local Community 26

GUIDELINES

A committee consisting of criminal justice personal will implement specific community notification guidelines. The guidelines provide for levels of notification based on the risk that a particular sex offender poses to the community. Level three poses a high risk to re-offend. Level two an intermediate and level one is a low risk.

The level three offenders require notification to the surrounding neighborhood, area schools, appropriate community groups, and offender prospective employer and the County Prosecutor or District Attorney Officer. A flyer will include a photo of the offender's status and criminal background. Also, the prior information is placed on the Internet. If a level three offender fails to register, a warrant is issued and the community is notified. The County Prosecutor or District Attorney will prosecute the offender for the failure to register.

The level two offenders, the notification may be make to the immediate neighbors, schools, appropriate community groups and prospective employers.

If the offender fails to register, the County District Attorney or the County Prosecutor will prosecute the offender.

The level one offender, the local law enforcement agency is responsible for the notification and shall maintain information about the offender. Information may be forwarded to the people with whom the offender resides. Once again, failure to register, the offender will be prosecuted.

SUMMARY

Sexual assault has been an instrumental rallying point in the growth of the victim movement in the United States. Many of these issues led to the revision of the criminal justice system to become more protective of victims. Sexual assault victims suffer a great deal of emotional trauma and endure a burdensome recovery process. In order to expedite the healing, new legislation and intervention have emerged. Although there has been major revisions in the enacted legislation, we need to continue the research and improve the training for criminal justice and related others to assist in the curtailing a very serious societal problem.

CHAPTER ASSIGNMENT

Obtain a copy of your state's sexual assault statute. Is your state statute more comprehensive or less inclusive than the previous discussed materials. List the changes:

_____
_____
_____
_____
_____
_____
_____
_____
_____
_____
_____
_____
_____
_____
_____
_____
_____
_____
_____
_____
_____
_____
_____
_____
_____
_____
_____

CHAPTER FIFTEEN

VICTIM ASSISTANT – STALKING

INTRODUCTION

Stalking behavior has existed since the commencement of time. However, this behavior had never been labeled as a distinct pattern of deviant social behavior and let alone a crime. It was not until the passage of the first anti-stalking statute in 1990, which such behavior became illegal. Since this event, legislators, criminal justice professionals, and victim service providers have started to examine the nature and psychological motivations behind stalking behavior. The studies of stalking and the development of effective response strategies is a discipline that is very much in its infancy. There appears to be numerous issues and challenges are being evolved on a daily basis. The rapid evolution of this issue places ever-increasing demands on the field to remain current and how to best assist victims and respond effectively to stalkers.

OBJECTIVES

The students will be able to understand the following concepts when this chapter has been completed:

1. The definition of stalking.
2. The characteristics of stalkers and their victims.
3. The categories used to classify stalking cases.
4. The method and motives of stalkers.
5. The impact of stalking on victims.
6. Response strategies for victims being stalked.

DEFINITION OF CONCEPTS

1. Stalking: Any person who engages in an course of conduct directed at a specific person that places that person, or their family, in reasonable fear for their safety, is guilty of the crime of stalking.

2. Simple Obsession Stalking: Involves previous personal relationships – between husbands/wives, girlfriends/boyfriends, and domestic partners and etc. Power and control underlie most domestic violence cases.

3. Love Obsession Stalking: Stalkers seek to establish a personal relationship with the object of their obsession. Love obsession stalkers tend to have low self-esteem and the victims are individuals who have social statues, or standing in their field or profession.

4. Erotomania Stalking: Individuals are delusional and consequently, virtually all suffer from mental disorder – most often schizophrenia. They believe that such a relationship already existed.

5. Vengeance/Terrorism Stalking: Vengeance stalkers do not seek a personal relationship with their targets. They attempt to elicit a

particular response or a change of behavior from their victim. When vengeance is their prime motive, stalkers seek only to punish their victims for some wrong they perceive the victim has visited upon them. In other words, they are getting even with their enemies.

IMPACT ON VICTIMS

Stalking has a tremendous impact on the lives of those who are targeted. The following represents the signs of stalking – related stress:

1. Loss of sleep
2. Weight loss
3. Depression
4. Anxiety
5. Difficulty concentrating

Many stalking victims experience a loss of personal support systems at the very moment they need them the most. Victims usually turn to family, friends, and co-workers for help, guidance, and emotional support.

However, the victims find that their friends, co-workers, neighbors, and even their family members are unable to sustain levels of long-term support. In some cases, victims have been terminated by the unsympathetic employers unwilling to accommodate the special needs of the victim employees.

STRATEGIES FOR STALKING VICTIMS

The stalking victims should employ the following strategies:

1. Notify the local law enforcement department or the County Prosecutors or District Attorney's Office

All stalking incidents should be reported to the police. You should request each incident to be documented. Request a copy of the report from the reporting law enforcement agency. You must record the name of the law enforcement officer recording the incident.

1. Keep a Diary: Obtain the names and addresses of all witnesses. Complete and detail records are essential to the successful prosecution of stalking cases.

2. Obtain a Restraining Order: If you are related to the stalker by blood or marriage, or if you live together, you need to obtain or pursue a restraining, or protective order.

3. Record Telephone Conversations: Advise the stalker to stop calling you and hang up. Screen your calls. Write down the times and dates of

each call. Retain recorded messages and give them to law enforcement.

4. Take Photo's of the Stalker: You should take all photos of the stalker, but it must be done with safety. The photos should be time dated and it can be placed on the reverse side of the photo.

5. Retain All Correspondence: Make all copies of anything you receive from the stalker. Touching the letter as little as possible will preserve the fingerprints.

6. Inform Everyone: You must tell friends, co-workers, and neighbors. Also, you must provide or give to them a detail description of the stalker. Ask them to document each time the stalker is seen by them.[27]

VICTIMS OF IMMINENT DANGER

The primary goal of victims in imminent danger is to locate a safe place for him or herself. Safety can be found in the subsequent places:

1. Law enforcement departments.
2. Residence of family or friends, especially if the location is not known to the stalker.
3. Domestic violence shelter/churches.
4. Public areas, stalkers are less inclined to commit acts of violence when the public can view the incident.

PREVENTIVE MEASURES

You should utilize the following preventive measures in order to insure your safety:

1. Install deadbolts.
2. Install adequate outside lighting.
3. Park securely in well lit areas.
4. Vary routes of travel.
5. Be alert and aware of your surroundings.
6. Have co-workers screen calls.
7. Maintain an unlisted telephone number.
8. If residing in an apartment, provide the manager with a picture of the suspect. [28]
9. Develop a safety plan for yourself and family in case of an emergency.

SUMMARY

Stalking is one of the most difficult issues facing criminal justice officials and victim service professionals. It has noted that stalking is far more common then previously estimated and its consequences to victims are more profound than imagined. The complexity of stalking behavior and the motivations behind such crimes make it a problem as difficult to comprehend as it is to solve. Professionals in the fields of criminology, psychology, and victimology have commenced to develop response strategies based on their initial study of experience with stalkers and stalking behavior. Only a comprehensive and coordinated response of committed individuals and institutions – both inside and outside the criminal justice system. It will likely succeed in stemming the fear, violence, and death that stalking inflicts on numerous victims each year.

CHAPTER ASSIGNMENT

You are required to develop a checklist for the establishment of an Anti-stalking Preventative Kit:

1. _____

2. _____

3. _____

4. _____

5. _____

6. _____

7. _____

8. _____

9. _____

10. _____

CHAPTER SIXTEEN

VICTIM ASSISTANCE - DRUNK DRIVING

INTRODUCTION

You may know someone who drinks and drives. You are in a difficult situation and may have some strong feelings about it. You care about the person but hate his or her drinking. You feel angry about irresponsible decisions made. You may live in terror of the moment you hear that this person has been injured or killed in a drunk driving crash or has been injured or killed by someone else.

Moreover, drunk driving is the most frequently committed violent crime in the United States. Millions of people know what it is like to care about someone who drinks and drives. We believe the information will provide guidance to you as you are coping with this person's drinking and driving problems.

Sorry to say, there is no magic solution to the problem. A strategy that works in one situation may no work in another.

OBJECTIVES

The student will be able to ascertain the following concepts:

1. Will be able to understand the importance of the concept called impaired.

2. Will be introduced to the BAC concepts and its meaning to the legal levels of intoxication.

3. Will be able to understand the consequences of drinking and driving.

4. Identify the notable symptoms of being intoxicated.

5. Discuss the changes of an alcoholic and its impact on his or her behavior. [29]

DEFINITION OF CONCEPTS

1. Impaired: impairment is the point where one's intake of alcohol or other drugs affects their ability to perform appropriately.

2. Intoxication: is a legal term that establishes a certain level of alcohol in the blood.

3. BAC: The blood alcohol content (BAC) which measures the number of grams of alcohol in your millimeters of blood.

4. MADD: Mothers Against Drunk Driving is a national organization assisting victims or survivors of drunk driving.

ALCOHOLISM AND THE ALCOHOLIC

Alcoholism is an embarrassing subject for some people. You may be very uncomfortable with the idea that someone you care about could be an alcoholic. An alcoholic is physically and/or psychologically addicted to alcohol. Alcoholism is believed by many to be a disease. If untreated, the alcoholic will rely more and more on alcohol to function and may ultimately die of the disease. Unlike some diseases, alcoholism also affects the family and friends of the alcoholic. Unless they've lived with the alcoholic, it's very difficult for other people to understand the emotional pain alcoholism can cause. Alcoholics are often wonderful people when they are sober.

Research has revealed the subsequent information regarding alcoholism:

1. Alcoholics tend to blame other people and situations for their drinking. The fact is, alcoholics drink because they are addicted.

2. Alcoholics cannot stop drinking without assistance. Therefore, it is very important that you seek assistance from someone familiar with helping alcoholics and their families.

3. Men, women and children of all ages and races can become alcoholics.

4. Alcoholism becomes worse without intervention and is usually ultimately fatal.

5. Nothing you can do or say will make the alcoholic stop drinking. It is the alcoholic who must make the decision.

CO-ALCOHOLICS

Co-alcoholic or co-dependent, or enabler is articulates the entire family is being affected by the problem of alcoholism, and in many cases, contributes to it. People who live with alcoholics tend to take on attitudes and behaviors they believe will help. The alcoholic maintains the addiction because other people support the behaviors of the alcoholics.

114

The co-dependents exhibit the following behaviors:

1. Lying or covering up for the alcoholic when he or she misses work, school or other obligations.

2. Hiding or throwing away alcohol or trying to monitor the alcoholic's amount of drinking.

3. Bailing the alcoholic out of jail or trouble caused by the drinking.

4. Denying to friends and family the alcoholic and themselves the severity of the problems.

5. Imagining that they are responsible for causing or curing the disease.

ALTERNATIVES TO DRINKING AND DRIVING

1. Designated Driver: A simple and effective alternative to impaired driving is to develop a plan before drinking. A designated driver is a person who agrees not to use alcohol or other drugs.

2. Public Transportation: If a group does not have a designated driver, drinkers should plan to use public transportation. Most bars and restaurants are more than happy to call a cab for their patrons.

3. Your Home: When the drinker is in your home and needs to go somewhere else, develop a transportation plan with him or her prior to the drinking starts. If all else fails, hide the keys, let the air out of the tires or even move the tires.

If you provide the alcohol, you may be legally liable if someone leaving your home injures or kills himself or someone else while driving. Making sure the drinker does not drive protects not only the drinkers, but other people on the road, and you.

MADD VICTIM IMPACT PANELS

MADD conducts Victim Impact Panels throughout the United States. The panels will include four or five victims of drunk driving who simply tell their stories. Audiences are made up of convicted first time drunk driving offenders who are required to attend as an element or requirement of their sentence. However, most panels are open to the public. To find out the location of the nearest panel, call your local MADD chapter or the National Office at 1-800-GET-MADD.

VICTIMS RIGHTS

The victims of drunk drivers have rights and they are as follows:

1. Advance notification on request of relevant court proceedings, including cancellations and rescheduling.

2. Information about the Crime Victims Compensation Fund and, on request, referral to social service agencies that provide that type of assistance.

3. Provide pertinent information concerning the impact of the crime to the probation department or related agency conducting the pre-sentence investigation.

4. Be present at all public court proceedings with the presiding judge's consent.

5. A safe waiting area at all public court proceedings.

6. Prompt return of any property that is no longer needed as evidence.

7. Complete a Victim Impact Statement, detailing the emotional, physical, and financial impact of the crime on the victim.

8. Information, on request, about parole proceedings, notification of parole proceedings and of the inmate's release and the right to participate in the parole process. [30]

SUMMARY

Drinking and driving remains a major problem and recent studies reveal that a majority of the public have admitted to driving after drinking too much or they rode with an impaired driver.

Moreover, the nation has experienced the largest percentage increase in alcohol-related traffic deaths on record.

Finally, alcohol-related traffic deaths are on the rise and especially with the under aged drinking levels reaching a plateau. We need to help keep our roadways safe and continue to support victims of drunken-drivers. Most important, we have to respond to the T.V. network's irresponsible decisions to air liquor ads and to assist in the development of standard for all alcohol advertisement.

CHAPTER ASSIGNMENT

You are required to complete the subsequent alcohol related questionnaire:
Does the person:

1. Need a drink at a certain time each day? _____

_____

_____

2. Drink alone or try to hide the drinking? _____

_____

_____

3. Deny that there's a problem or get upset if you complain
about the drinking? _____

_____

_____

4. Have frequent illnesses or injuries that may be related to
the drinking? _____

_____

_____

5. Lose time from work or school because of the drinking?

_____

_____

6. Experience memory loss or loss of control while or after
drinking? _____

_____

_____

7. Become angry, jealous or violent after drinking? _____

_____

_____

8. Feel guilty, depressed or ashamed of the drinking? ____

_____

_____

9. Limit social activity strictly to friends and events that
involve drinking? _____

_____

_____

Answering yes to any of these questions may indicate that the
person is a problem drinker or an alcoholic. It's important that you get help.

CHAPTER SEVENTEEN

RESTORATIVE JUSTICE AND RECONCILIATION

INTRODUCTION

The victim's movement has been traveling on the avenue called success and they have been gaining a greater influence on how cases are resolved within the criminal justice system. There are numerous advocacy groups who want to empower victims so they can be treated with a sense of fundamental fairness. However, there are others who are moving away from the formal legal rights to the exploration of informal alternatives. There are two opposite theories; one leads the participants on a quest for non-legalistic and non-adversarial ways to resolve differences between individuals that have entailed themselves in conflicts. This is called restorative justice and the other is the victim-offender reconciliation is the goal. Moreover, restitution is arranged through the mediator method which the setting will be neighborhood justice center or at a community-based program.

OBJECTIVES

After reading this chapter, you should be able to:

1. Summarize the goals of the victim-offender reconciliation programs.

2. Explain the philosophy of the restorative justice programs.

3. Understand the importance of the mediator.

4. Describe the critical stages of reconciliation.

5. Define restitution and its importance to the victim and the community.

DEFINITION OF CONCEPTS

1. Restitution: the repayment of monetary funds or the performance of services to the victim or the community.

2. Mediator: a non-partial party who hears concerns from both sides and attempts to encourage the parties to resolve or settle their indifferences.

3. Victim Impact Statements: the victim is given the opportunity to inform the court or related criminal justice agency his or her emotional, physical and financial cost associated with the victimization.

RESTORATIVE JUSTICE

The restorative justice is attracting a growing proportion of victims who don't want to utilize their leverage within the legal system to make their offenders suffer. They are taking advantage of the chance to actively participate in a process whose goals are offender sensitization, victim recovery, a cessation of mutual hostilities and a sense of closure, in which both parties put the incident behind them and rebuild their lives. It draws upon non-punitive methods of peacemaking, mediation, negotiation, dispute resolution, conflict management and constructive engagement. These tactics are employed to bring about mutual understanding, offender empathy for the victim's plight sensitivity for the cause of offender's crime-inducing problems, and lasting settlements that reconcile tensions between the two parties as well as within their community. Restorative justice embraces themes important to the victim rights movement, especially empowerment, notification, direct involvement, offender accountability, and achieving restitution.

Some restorative justice projects have experimented with two traditional ways of bringing the various estranged parties together, peacemaking circles and family group conferencing. The use of the overlapping peacemaking circles composed of the victim and his or her support system, the offender and his or her family, and community members is derived from Native American tribal culture in the United States and Canada. The community, the victim and the offender all need to be intimately involved in dealing with the problem and solutions. By doing so, society is supposed to become a better place for everyone, not just the immediate victim and offender.

Restorative justice involves various constituencies. Under this approach, the victims are compensated through restitution, and they are given a greater voice in the case handling and become an integral part of the treatment or intervention provided to the offender. The offender is held accountable for his or her transgressions and may be subjected to a variety of possible interventions. These may include incarceration, restitution orders, meetings with the victims, involvement in rehabilitation programs; such as educational or vocational training, drug treatment and or community service work. The offender makes amends and is assisted in order to mitigate the chances of future deviance. Finally, the government or the criminal justice system is to provide fair and equitable procedures for all parties. In essence, restorative justice seeks to bring all parties to the table in a mutual assistance pact. Everyone who comes in with a need is to deport with some degree of satisfaction. 31

RECONCILIATION

The reconciliation process is a desired outcome that has four distinct phases:
1. Case Selection,
2. Preparation,
3. Mediation and Negotiation,
4. Monitoring during the follow-up period.

The healing process begins when a case manager sorts out ones that appear to be suitable. Next, a trained mediator contacts the complainant and then the accused in order to explain the mechanics of the program. Is it important to discuss the nature of the charges, and test their willingness to participate in a face-to-face encounter. If the parties agree, the mediator meets with each side separately and brings the two disputants together. At their conference or dialogue meeting, both parties vent their emotions and share their reactions to the crime and the way the criminal justice system handled the case. They attempt to resolve their differences in a mutual and acceptable manner, in which the offender pledges restitution to cover the victims expenses. Subsequent to the meeting, the mediator remains in contact with both parties, supervising and verifying that the written contract is being completely fulfilled. The agreement requires the wrongdoer to make payments from earnings or under take the completion of the community service work schedule.

The heart of the process is the encounter between the victim and the offender in a structured and secure setting: Program's headquarters, or in a house of worship. Usually, each side has already met satisfied with the mediator. The mediator is an uncertified volunteer with at least 30 hours of training and experience. The mediator will attempt to make the parties feel comfortable in order to facilitate their dialogue.

Eventually, the wrongdoer (offender) experiences genuine remorse and offers to apologize to the victim. The mediator, program staff or a probation officer supervises the repayment process during the follow-up period.

The majority of victim-offender reconciliation programs are ran by a private non-profit organization rather than the criminal justice system agencies. [32]

SUMMARY

The victim movement is maturing. There have been a substantial number of initiatives to provide victims with rights. The law covers a wide range of areas, such restitution, victim compensation, victim impact statements and the notification of system procedures. This suggests that victim rights will continue to gain even more performance.

It is important to seek an equitable balance. In the past, the system had erred by becoming overly concerned with offender's rights. The same statement can be made about the victim's rights arena if the appropriate precautionary steps are not taken.

ASSIGNMENT

1. What will restorative justice accomplish? _____

_____

_____

_____

_____

_____

_____

_____

_____

_____

_____

_____

_____

_____

_____

_____

_____

_____

2. Contact your Prosecutor or District Attorney Office to learn whether said office utilizes the Restorative Justice or The Victim-Offender Reconciliation Programs. If such an alternative is in use, inquire as to whether you can attend such matter and outline the steps of the program. _____

_____

_____

_____

_____

_____

_____

_____

_____

_____

_____

_____

_____

_____

CHAPTER EIGHTEEN

TRENDS AND VISION

INTRODUCTION

This chapter has been designed to examine the trends the field of victimology may travel. It will show you the changing and evolving of the retaliatory justice approaches, as an answer to the victim who believes that he or she must fight in order to retain his or her dignity and respect.

Moreover, the chapter will envision the various types of pedophilias and the abuse of the clergy or the church abuser breaking the band of trust.

OBJECTIVES

After reading this chapter, you will be able to:

1. Define the pedophilia.
2. Explain the retaliatory justice concept.
3. Identify vigilantism and its role in the emerging of the law.
4. Distinguish between punitive and necessary rationales.

DEFINITION OF CONCEPTS

1. Pedophilia: An adult child molester.

2. Vigilantism: The outlaw alternative to formal case processing, or the do-it-yourself approach to retaliating against the attacker.

3. Punitive Rationale: Using force against an attacker because the aggressor needs to suffer for the wrongdoings.

4. Necessity Rationale: Victim doesn't have to yield his or her territory as a means of self-protection.

5. Individualistic Rationale: Victim doesn't need to confront the attacker when he or she approaches.

6. Right-to-Carry Statutes: Statutes that enables the ordinary citizen to carry concealed handguns during their daily activities.

7. Police Vigilantism: Commonly referred to as police brutality.

RETALIATORY JUSTICE

There is another kind of informal justice that has little in common with the peacemaking that is offered at mediation programs. It is entirely a different type of conflict resolution that relies on the use of force, not negotiation and compromise. It has a long history of blood and killings that are retaliatory. This outlawed alternative embodies the do-it-yourself approach. To the criminal justice system, it is the modern-day expression of that old fashioned impulse called vigilantism. Examples of retaliatory actions are when a victim's family members or friends take actions against the offender.

Over the course of American history, vigilantism has often arisen as a response to victimization. Vigilantism called for action whenever honest upright citizens become enraged and terrified about what they considered to be upsurge of criminality and a breakdown of law and order. 33

PEDOPHILIA

The studies reveal that the pedophiles have been compared to the alcoholics. They may be treatable, but not curable in their present condition. The treatment can help them control their sexual urges toward children.

There are three major types of pedophiles. They are as follows:

> 1. Intimate: Usually they cultivate a relationship with the children they later molest.
>
> 2. Aggressive: Are ones who use violence and force.
>
> 3. Opportunistic Criminal: Are ones who commit a variety of crimes:
>> a) Burglary
>> b) Rape
>> c) Assault
>> d) Sexual Assault upon a child

Many pedophiles are very immature, childish, and do very poorly in social situations.

Pedophiles can be attracted to either boys or girls and while most pedophiles are men but women can be sexually attracted to children.

Pedophiles have included some prominent people. Lewis Carroll, author of "Alice Adventures in Wonderland," and Sir James Barric, author of "Peter Pan," are cited by forensic psychologists as likely pedophiles.

The Nobel Prize winner, Daniel Carleton Gajdusek, a pediatrician and researcher was jailed in 1997 for molesting a 16-year-old boy, one of 56 children he brought back from over seas.

The pedophiles are very similar to the alcoholic, the recovering alcoholic have to stay away from places where drinks may tempt them, so pedophiles need to avoid places where they will be tempted by the presence of children.

Celibacy does not contribute to the problem, although some people may go into the priesthood and take a vow of celibacy believing it will help them avoid their desires toward children.

CHURCH ABUSE

Some spiral into suicide or lonely despair, others become articulate crusaders for change and are supported by loving families. The common bond for victims of sexual abuse by clergymen is a piercing sense of betrayal.

There are hundreds of abused victims who have joined SNAP - Survivors Network of those Abused by Priests. The group was founded in 1991, offering emotional support to victims and it monitors responses of church officials to abuse scandals, such as the Boston Roman Catholic community.

Parishioners know that a priest has these magical functions to bring Christ's presence to them. The victim believes that the priest who abuses you is abusing of your soul. Victims live a life of tremendous shame, thinking that they've had sex with God.

There are thousands of victims throughout the United States who have been abused by the priests. The abuse breaks the bond of trust, but the Church as to confront the numerous problems that it has incurred. [34]

SUMMARY

An academic examination of the revenge killings and other acts of vigilantism leads victimology full circle, back to its ancestral origins in criminology. In trying to vindicate victims, vigilantes create new ones.

The final trends or visions of pedophiles and the abuse of the priests have articulated the last theme developed regarding the concerns involved with informal victim participation. The final chapter closes with a plea for transforming the current operation into a justice system as opposed to the criminal justice system.

CHAPTER NINETEEN

GRANTS

CHAPTER NINETEEN: GRANTS

This chapter has been implemented to inform the students of the vast directory of grants. These grants have been funded by the Office for Victims of Crime of the U.S. Department of Justice. The OVC administers formula and discretionary grants diverse victim services throughout the United States. The Grants directory commences with the State of Alabama coupled with the various grant programs and the same. The grants will provide excellent resources or seed funding when organizations are in need of funds to commence victim assistance programs or community victim programs.

GRANTS

The Office for Victims of Crime: U.S. Department of Justice
Office of Justice Programs
810 Seventh Street NW
Washington, DC 20531

The OVC is a federal agency located within the Office of Justice Programs of the US Department of Justice (DOJ) that Congress formally established in 1988 through an amendment to the 1984 Victims of Crime Act (VOCA). OVC provides federal leadership and federal funds to support victim compensation and assistance programs around the country and advocates for the fair treatment of crime victims worldwide. OVC administers formula and discretionary grants designed to benefit victims, provides training for diverse professionals who work with victims, develops projects to enhance victims' rights and services, and undertakes public education and awareness activities on behalf of crime victims. OVC accomplishes its work through the following divisions:

State Compensation and Assistance Division – This division administers formula grants for local and state crime victim compensation and assistance programs. Approximately 90 percent of the money deposited into the Crime Victims Fund each year is distributed through this division.

Special Projects Division – As the program development arm of OVC, this division establishes national-scope training, technical assistance, and demonstration programs; launches special initiatives that address major issues in the victims field, and provides education about crime victim issues.

Federal Crime Victims Division – Through this division, OVC works to provide federal crime victims with assistance and full participation in the criminal justice process. The division distributes funds to federal criminal justice agencies and American Indian Tribes and Alaskan Natives across the country to support training and direct services for victims.

Technical Assistance, Publications, and Information Resources Unit – This division manages the OVC Resource Center, the OVC Training and Technical Assistance Center, education and outreach initiatives, and the publication and dissemination of OVC materials and grant products.

Terrorism and International Victims Unit – OVC's newest unit develops programs and initiatives to help victims of terrorism and mass violence and victims of crimes involving transnational dimensions, such as victimization of tourists, trafficking of adults and children for exploitative purposes, and international child abduction. [35]

ALABAMA

Edward Byrne Formula Grant
Jim Quinn
Phone: (334) 242-5811
Fax: (334) 242-0712
jimq@adeca.state.al.us

Family Violence Prevention and Services Act
Jim Quinn
Phone: (334) 242-5811
Fax: (334) 242-0712
jimq@adeca.state.al.us

STOP Violence Against Women Act
Jim Quinn
Phone: (334) 242-5811
Fax: (334) 242-0712

VOCA Victim Assistance
Jim Quinn
Phone: (334) 242-5811
Fax: (334) 242-0712
jimq@adeca.state.al.us

VOCA Victim Compensation
Martin Ramsay
Phone: (334) 242-4007
Fax: (334) 353-1401
mramsay@acvcc.state.al.us

Children's Justice Act
Phyllis Matthews
Phone: (334) 242-1468
Fax: (334) 353-1052
pmatthews@dhr.state.al.us

Office for State and Local Domestic Preparedness Support
Lee Helms
Phone: (205) 280-2201
Fax: (205) 280-2410
leeh@aema.state.al.us

ALASKA

Edward Byrne Formula Grant
Catherine Katsel
Phone: (907) 269-5082
Fax: (907) 337-2059
pckatsel@psafety.state.ak.us

Family Violence Prevention and Services Act
Trisha Gentle
Phone: (907) 465-4322
Fax: (907) 465-4362

STOP Violence Against Women Act
Trisha Gentle
Phone: (907) 465-4356
Fax: (907) 465-3627

VOCA Victim Assistance
Trisha Gentle
Phone: (907) 465-5504
Fax: (907) 465-3627
Trisha_gentle@dps.state.ak.us

VOCA Victim Compensation
Susan Browne
Phone: (800) 764-3040
Fax: (907) 465-2379
Susan_browne@dps.state.ak.us

Children's Justice Ace
Ellen Ritzman
Phone: (907) 465-3458
Fax: (907) 465-3656
Ellen_ritzman@health.state.ak.us

Office for State and Local Domestic Preparedness Support
Wayne Rush
Phone: (907) 428-7032
Fax: (907) 428-7009
waynerush@ak-prepared.com

ARIZONA

Edward Byrne Formula Grant
Joseph R. Farmer
Phone: (602) 230-0252
Fax: (602) 728-0752
acjc@goodnet.com (notify before sending)

Family Violence Prevention and Services Act
Ann Tarpy
Phone: (602) 542-7341
Fax: (602) 542-1062

STOP Violence Against Women Act
Donna Irwin
Phone: (602) 542-1764
Fax: (602) 542-5522

VOCA Victim Assistance
Jane Conder
Phone: (602) 223-2480
Fax: (602) 223-2943
jconder@dps.state.az.us

VOCA Victim Compensation
Donna Marcum
Phone: (602) 230-0252 x208
Fax: (602) 728-0752
dmarcum@acjc.state.az.us

Children's Justice Act
Beverly Ogden
Phone: (602) 331-8778
Fax: (602) 678-6939
beaogden@homel.com

Office for State and Local Domestic Preparedness Support
Linda Mason
Phone: (602) 231-6218
Fax: (602) 231-6206
masonl@dem.state.az.us

ARKANSAS

Edward Byrne Formula Grant
Randy Dennis
Phone: (501) 682-2579
Fax: (501) 682-5206
Randy.dennis@adga.state.ar.us

Family Violence Prevention and Services Act
Randy Dennis
Phone: (501) 682-5153
Fax: (501) 682-5155
Randy.dennis@adga.state.ar.us

STOP Violence Against Women Act
Ruth Parker
Phone: (501) 682-5149
Fax: (501) 682-5155

VOCA Victim Assistance
Ruth Parker
Phone: (501) 682-1074
Fax: (501) 682-5206

VOCA Victim Compensation
Kathy Sheehan
Phone: (501) 682-2656
Fax: (501) 682-5313
kathys@ag.state.ar.us

Children's Justice Act
Carol Griffin
Phone: (501) 661-7975
Fax: (501) 661-7967
Griffincarol@exchange.uams.edu

Office for State and Local Domestic Preparedness Support
Jack DuBose
Phone: (501) 730-9782
Fax: (501) 730-9778
jackdubose@adem.state.ar.us

CALIFORNIA

Edward Byrne Formula Grant
Carol Geber
Phone: (916) 323-7612
Fax: (916) 327-8714

Family Violence Prevention and Services Act
Harry Liddicote
Phone: (916) 324-9240
Fax: (916) 324-9167

STOP Violence Against Women Act
Maria Rubick
Phone: (916) 323-7736
Fax: (916) 324-8554

VOCA Victim Assistance
Maria Rubick
Phone: (916) 323-7736
Fax: (916) 324-9167
Mariaelena.rubick@ocjp.ca.gov

VOCA Victim Compensation
Skip Ellsworth
Phone: (916) 327-0394
Fax: (916) 327-2933
sellsworth@boc.ca.gov

Children's Justice Act
Lisa Fey-Williams
Phone: (916) 324-9190
Fax: (916) 324-8554
Lisa.fey-williams@ocjp.ca.gov

Office for State and Local Domestic Preparedness Support
Dallas Jones
Phone: (916) 262-1816
Fax: (916) 262-2837
dallasjones@oes.ca.gov

COLORADO

Edward Byrne Formula Grant
Lance Clem
Phone: (303) 239-5717
Fax: (303) 239-4491
Lance.clem@cdps.state.co.us

Family Violence Prevention and Services Act
Mary Ann Ganey
Phone: (303) 866-2855
Fax: (303) 866-4629

STOP Violence Against Women Act
Wendell Graham
Phone: (303) 239-5728
Fax: (303) 239-5743

VOCA Victim Assistance
Robert Gallup
Phone: (303) 239-4529
Fax: (303) 239-4411
Robert.gallup@cdps.state.ca.gov

VOCA Victim Compensation
Deborah Kasyon
Phone: (303) 239-4402
Fax: (303) 239-4411
Deborah.kasyon@cdps.state.co.us

Children's Justice Act
Janet Motz
Phone: (303) 866-5137
Fax: (303) 866-5563
Janet.motz@state.co.us

Office for State and Local Domestic Preparedness Support
Greg Moser
Phone: (303) 273-1640
Fax: (303) 273-1795
Greg.moser@state.oc.co.us

CONNECTICUT

Edward Byrne Formula Grant
Elizabeth Graham
Phone: (860) 418-6279
Fax: (860) 418-6496
Libby.graham@po.state.ct.us

Family Violence Prevention and Services Act
Joseph A. Freyre
Phone: (860) 424-5872
Fax: (860) 951-2996

STOP Violence Against Women Act
Lisa Secondo
Phone: (860) 418-6391
Fax: (860) 418-6496

VOCA Victim Assistance
Linda Cimino
Phone: (860) 747-6070
Fax: (860) 747-6428
Linda.cimino@jud.state.ct.us

VOCA Victim Compensation
Linda Cimino
Phone: (860) 747-6070
Fax: (860) 747-6428
Linda.cimino@jud.state.ct.us

Children's Justice Act
Catherine Ewing-Rinker
Phone: (860) 550-6607
Fax: (860) 560-6541
Catherine.ewing-rinker@po.state.ct.us

Office for State and Local Domestic Preparedness Support
Greg Chiara
Phone: (860) 566-3376
Fax: (860) 247-0664
Gregory.chiara@po.state.ct.us

DELAWARE

Edward Byrne Formula Grant
Joe Pennell
Phone: (302) 577-5030
Fax: (302) 577-3440

Family Violence Prevention and Services Act
Corrine Pearson
Phone: (302) 577-3697
Fax: (302) 577-3440

STOP Violence Against Women Act
Maureen Querey
Phone: (302) 577-5025
Fax: (302) 577-3440

VOCA Victim Assistance
Corrine Pearson
Phone: (302) 577-8696
Fax: (302) 577-3440
coPearson@state.de.us

VOCA Victim Compensation
Joseph Hughes
Phone: (302) 995-8383
Fax: (302) 995-8387

Children's Justice Act
Kevin Odwin
Phone: (302) 633-2660
Fax: (302) 633-2652
kodwin@state.de.us

Office for State and Local Domestic Preparedness Support
Sean Mulhern
Phone: (302) 659-3362
Fax: (302) 659-6855
jmulhern@state.de.us

FLORIDA

Edward Byrne Formula Grant
Clayton Wilder
Phone: (850) 410-8700
Fax: (850) 410-8728

Family Violence Prevention and Services Act
Trula E. Motta
Phone: (850) 488-8762

STOP Violence Against Women Act
Pat Barrett
Phone: (850) 414-8312
Fax: (850) 922-6720

VOCA Victim Assistance
Christina Frank
Phone: (850) 414-3340
Fax: (850) 487-3013
Christina_frank@oag.state.fl.us

VOCA Victim Compensation
Gwen Roache
Phone: (904) 414-3300
Fax: (904) 487-1595
Gwen_roache@oag.state.fl.us

Children's Justice Act
Jim Spencer
Phone: (850) 487-2006
Fax: (850) 921-2038
Jim_spencer@dcf.state.fl.us

Office for State and Local Domestic Preparedness Support
W. Craig Fugate
Phone: (850) 413-9837
Fax: (850) 488-5777
Craig.fugate@dca.state.fl.us

GEORGIA

Edward Byrne Formula Grant
Joe Hood
Phone: (404) 559-4949 x116
Fax: (404) 5594960

Family Violence Prevention and Services Act
Cheryl M. Christian
Phone: (404) 657-3423
Fax: (404) 657-3489

STOP Violence Against Women Act
LaSonja Fillingame
Phone: (404) 559-4949
Fax: (404) 559-4960

VOCA Victim Assistance
Joe Hood III
Phone: (404) 559-4949
Fax: (404) 559-4960
jhood@cjcc.state.ga.us

VOCA Victim Compensation
Shawanda Reynolds-Cobb
Phone: (404) 559-4949
Fax: (404) 559-4960
sreynold@cjcc.state.ga.us

Children's Justice Act
Sarah G. Brownlee
Phone: (404) 657-3463
Fax: (404) 657-4483
sgbrownl@dhr.state.ga.us

Office for State and Local Domestic Preparedness Support
V. Bartlett
Phone: (404) 635-7002
Fax: (404) 635-7205
vbartlett@gema.state.ga.us

HAWAII

Edward Byrne Formula Grant
Lari Koga
Phone: (808) 586-1151
Fax: (808) 586-1373
akwock@laba.net

Family Violence Prevention and Services Act
David Boemer
Phone: (808) 586-5664
Fax: (808) 586-5700

STOP Violence Against Women Act
Tony Wong
Phone: (808) 586-1282
Fax: (808) 586-1373

VOCA Victim Assistance
Adrian Kwock
Phone: (808) 586-1155
Fax: (808) 586-1373
akwock@lava.net

VOCA Victim Compensation
Pamela Serguson-Brey
Phone: (808) 587-1143
Fax: (808) 587-1146
Psserguson-Brey@lava.net

Children's Justice Act
Gibby Fukutomi
Phone: (808) 586-5702
Fax: (808) 586-5606
gibbyf@hotmail.com

Office for State and Local Domestic Preparedness Support
Kelvin Ogata
Phone: (808) 733-4301
Fax: (808) 733-4248
kogata@scd.state.hi.us

IDAHO

Edward Byrne Formula Grant
Roberta Silva
Phone: (208) 884-7040
Fax: (208) 884-7094
Roberts.silva@isp.state.id.us

Family Violence Prevention and Services Act
Celia V. Heady
Phone: (208) 334-5580
Fax: (208) 332-7353

STOP Violence Against Women Act
Steve Raschke
Phone: (208) 884-7042
Fax: (208) 884-7094

VOCA Victim Assistance
Celia V. Heady
Phone: (208) 334-5580
Fax: (208) 332-7353
cheady@icdv.state.id.us

VOCA Victim Compensation
George Gutierrez
Phone: (208) 334-6070
Fax: (208) 334-5145
ggutierr@iic.state.id.us

Children's Justice Act
Shirley Alexander
Phone: (208) 334-6618
Fax: (208) 334-6664
alexande@idhw.state.id.us

Office for State and Local Domestic Preparedness Support
Bill Bishop
Phone: (208) 334-3263
Fax: (208) 334-3267
bbishop@bds.state.id.us

ILLINOIS

Edward Byrne Formula Grant
Robert Taylor
Phone: (312) 793-8550
Fax: (312) 793-8422
Taylor@icjia.state.il.us

Family Violence Prevention and Services Act
Carol Brigman
Phone: (217) 524-6034
Fax: (217) 524-6029

STOP Violence Against Women Act
Robert Taylor
Phone: (312) 793-8550
Fax: (312) 793-8422

VOCA Victim Assistance
Robert Taylor
Phone: (312) 793-8550
Fax: (312) 793-8422
rtaylor@icjia.state.il.us

VOCA Victim Compensation
Martha Newton
Phone: (312) 814-2581
Fax: (312) 814-5079
Mnewton@stg.state.il.us

Children's Justice Act
Cheryl Peterson
Phone: (217) 785-0014
Fax: (217) 785-9454
cpeterso@idcfs.state.il.us

Office for State and Local Domestic Preparedness Support
Mike Chamness
Phone: (212) 782-2700
Fax: (212) 557-4783
rcoble@iema.state.il.us

INDIANA

Edward Byrne Formula Grant
Doug Fowler
Phone: (317) 232-1230
Fax: (317) 232-4979

Family Violence Prevention and Services Act
Lena Harris
Phone: (317) 232-4241
Fax: (317) 232-4436

STOP Violence Against Women Act
Melissa Moland
Phone: (317) 232-1233
Fax: (317) 232-4979

VOCA Victim Assistance
Gregory Hege
Phone: (317) 233-3383
Fax: (317) 232-4979
ghege@cji.state.in.us

VOCA Victim Compensation
Gregory Hege
Phone: (317) 233-3383
Fax: (317) 232-4979
ghege@cji.state.in.us

Office for State and Local Domestic Preparedness Support
Phil Roberts
Phone: (317) 232-3834
Fax: (317) 232-3895
proberts@sema.state.in.us

IOWA

Edward Byrne Formula Grant
Dale R. Woolery
Phone: (515) 281-3788
Fax: (515) 242-6390

Family Violence Prevention and Services Act
Virginia Beane
Phone: (515) 281-5044
Fax: (515) 281-8199

STOP Violence Against Women Act
Rebecca Kinnamon
Phone: (515) 242-6379
Fax: (515) 242-6390

VOCA Victim Assistance
Virginia Beane
Phone: (515) 281-5044
Fax: (515) 281-8199
vbeane@ag.state.ia.us

VOCA Victim Compensation
Julie Swanston
Phone: (515) 281-5044
Fax: (515) 281-8199
jswanst@ag.state.ia.us

Children's Justice Act
Wayne McCracken
Phone: (515) 281-8978
Fax: (515) 242-6884
wmccrac@dhs.state.ia.us

Office for State and Local Domestic Preparedness Support
Ellen Gordon
Phone: (515) 281-3231
Fax: (515) 281-7539
Ellen.Gordon@emd.state.ia.us

KANSAS

Edward Byrne Formula Grant
Carla Campbell
Phone: (785) 296-0923
Fax: (785) 296-0927
Carla@CJNetworks.com

Family Violence Prevention and Services Act
Juliene Maska
Phone: (785) 296-3131

STOP Violence Against Women Act
Juliene Maska
Phone: (785) 296-2215
Fax: (785) 296-6296

VOCA Victim Assistance
Juliene Maska
Phone: (785) 296-2215
Fax: (785) 296-6296
maskaj@ksag.org

VOCA Victim Compensation
Frank Henderson, Jr.
Phone: (785) 296-2359
Fax: (785) 296-0652
hendersf@at02po.wpo.state.ks.us

Children's Justice Act
Patti Dawson
Phone: (785) 368-8153
Fax: (785) 368-8159
pad@srskansas.org

Office for State and Local Domestic Preparedness Support
Tim Lockett
Phone: (785) 296-6800
Fax: (785) 296-3049
tlockett@mail.khp.state.ks.us

KENTUCKY

Edward Byrne Formula Grant
Debra McGovern
Phone: (502) 564-7554
Fax: (502) 564-4840
Debra.McGovern@mail.state.ky.us

Family Violence Prevention and Services Act
Cliff Jennings
Phone: (502) 564-7536
Fax: (502) 564-2467

STOP Violence Against Women Act
Donna Langley
Phone: (502) 564-3251
Fax: (502) 564-4840

VOCA Victim Assistance
Donna Langley
Phone: (502) 564-3251
Fax: (502) 564-5244
dlangley@mail.state.ky.us

VOCA Victim Compensation
Sheila Tharpe
Phone: (502) 564-7986
Fax: (502) 564-4817
Sheila.tharpe@mail.state.ky.us

Children's Justice Act
Carol C. Wilson
Phone: (502) 564-2136
Fax: (502) 564-3096
Carolc.Wilson@mail.state.ky.us

Office for State and Local Domestic Preparedness Support
W. R. Padgett
Phone: (502) 607-1689
Fax"   (502) 607-1251
rpadgett@kyds.dma.state.ky.us

LOUISIANA

Edward Byrne Formula Grant
Tolly Thompson
Phone: (225) 925-4942
Fax: (225) 925-1998
Michael@cole.state.la.us

Family Violence Prevention and Services Act
Eleanor Shirley
Phone: (504) 922-0960
Fax: (504) 922-0959

STOP Violence Against Women Act
Ronald Schulingkamp
Phone: (225) 925-1757
Fax: (225) 925-1998

VOCA Victim Assistance
Ronald Schulingkamp
Phone: (225) 925-1757
Fax: (225) 925-1998
ronalds@cole.state.la.us

VOCA Victim Compensation
Bob Wertz
Phone: (225) 925-4437
Fax: (225) 925-1998
bobw@cole.state.la.us

Children's Justice Act
Isabel Wingerter
Phone: (225) 342-9639
Fax: (225) 342-9637
wingerteri@ag.state.la.us

Office for State and Local Domestic Preparedness Support
Lt. Colonel Mark Oxley
Phone: (225) 922-2293
Fax: (225) 925-4903
moxley@dps.state.la.us

MAINE

Edward Byrne Formula Grant
David Giampetruzzi
Phone: (207) 624-7074
Fax: (207) 624-8768
David.a.giampetruzzi@state.me.us

Family Violence Prevention and Services Act
Jeannette Talbot
Phone: (207) 287-5060
Fax: (207) 287-5031

STOP Violence Against Women Act
Peter Brough
Phone: (207) 624-8756
Fax: (207) 624-8463

VOCA Victim Assistance
Jeannette Talbot
Phone: (207) 287-5060
Fax: (207) 287-5065
Jeannette.c.Talbot@state.me.us

VOCA Victim Compensation
Deborah Shaw Rice
Phone: (207) 626-8589
Fax: (207) 624-7730
Deb.rice@state.me.us

Children's Justice Act
Sandra Hodge
Phone: (207) 287-5060
Fax: (207) 287-5282
Sandra.s.hodge@state.me.us

Office for State and Local Domestic Preparedness Support
Lt. Craig Poulin
Phone: (207) 624-8988
Fax: (207) 624-8765
Craig.a.poulin@state.me.us

MARYLAND

Edward Byrne Formula Grant
Don Farabaugh
Phone: (410) 321-3521
Fax: (410) 321-3116
don@goccp-state-md.org

Family Violence Prevention and Services Act
Adrienne Siegel
Phone: (410) 767-7176
Fax: (410) 333-0256

STOP Violence Against Women Act
Pat Baker-Simon
Phone: (410) 321-3521 x356
Fax: (410) 321-3116

VOCA Victim Assistance
Adrienne Siegel
Phone: (410) 767-7176
Fax: (410) 333-0256
asiegel@dhr.state.md.us

VOCA Victim Compensation
Robin Woolford, Jr.
Phone: (410) 585-3042
Fax: (410) 764-4373
rwoolford@dpscs.state.mn.us

Children's Justice Act
Shirley Brown
Phone: (410) 767-7583
Fax: (410) 333-0127
sbrown@ssa.dhr.state.md.us

Office for State and Local Domestic Preparedness Support
Don Lumpkins
Phone: (410) 517-3618
Fax: (410) 517-3610
Dlumpkins@mema.state.md.us

MASSACHUSETTS

Edward Byrne Formula Grant
Jane Zuroff
Phone: (617) 727-6300
Fax: (617) 727-5356
Jane.zuroff@state.ma.us

Family Violence Prevention and Services Act
Pamela Whitney
Phone: (617) 727-3171
Fax: (617) 261-7435

STOP Violence Against Women Act
Marilee Kenney-Hunt
Phone: (617) 727-6300
Fax: (617) 727-5356

VOCA Victim Assistance
Brenda Noel
Phone: (617) 727-0115
Fax: (617) 727-6552
Brenda.noel@state.ma.us

VOCA Victim Compensation
Cheryl Watson
Phone: (617) 727-2200
Fax: (617) 367-3906
Cheryl.Watson@ago.state.ma.us

Children's Justice Act
Jan Carey
Phone: (617) 748-2328
Fax: (617) 261-7435
Jan.carey-DSS@state.ma.us

Office for State and Local Domestic Preparedness Support
Kathleen Estridge
Phone: (508) 820-2018
Fax: (508) 820-2030
kathleenestridge@state.ma.us

MICHIGAN

Edward Byrne Formula Grant
Ardith DaFoe
Phone: (517) 373-2952
Fax: (517) 373-2963
dafoea@state.mi.us

Family Violence Prevention and Services Act
Darlene Edington
Phone: (517) 373-7797
Fax: (517) 373-8471

STOP Violence Against Women Act
Deborah Cain
Phone: (517) 373-6388
Fax: (517) 241-8903

VOCA Victim Assistance
Leslie O'Reilly
Phone: (517) 373-1826
Fax: (517) 241-2769
OreillyL@state.mi.us

VOCA Victim Compensation
Michael Fullwood
Phone: (517) 373-0979
Fax: (517) 241-2769
fullwoodm@state.mi.us

Children's Justice Act
Lu DeLoach
Phone: (517) 373-9171
Fax: (517) 241-7047
KeLoachl@state.mi.us

Office for State and Local Domestic Preparedness Support
Edward Buikema
Phone: (517) 336-6157
Fax: (517) 336-6551
buikemaE@msp.msp-seoc

MINNESOTA

Edward Byrne Formula Grant
Jeri Boisvert
Phone: (651) 284-3318
Fax: (651) 582-8499

Family Violence Prevention and Services Act
Claudia Aherns
Phone: (651) 205-4821
Fax: (651) 296-5787

STOP Violence Against Women Act
Rachel Bandy
Phone: (651) 282-6256
Fax: (612) 296-5787

VOCA Victim Assistance
Jim Whittington
Phone: (651) 282-6267
Fax: (651) 205-4808

VOCA Victim Compensation
Marie Bibus
Phone: (651) 282-6267
Fax: (612) 296-5787
Marie.bibus@state.mn.us

Children's Justice Act
Sara Klise
Phone: (651) 296-0813
Fax: (651) 297-1949
Sara.klise@state.mn.us

Office for State and Local Domestic Preparedness Support
Kevin C. Leuer
Phone: (651) 296-0450
Fax: (651) 296-0459
Kevin.leuer@state.mn.us

MISSISSIPPI

Edward Byrne Formula Grant
Joyce Word
Phone: (601) 359-7880
Fax: (601) 359-7832

Family Violence Prevention and Services Act
Janet Howard
Phone: (601) 960-7470
Fax: (601) 960-7948
delrod@mail.state.mo.us

STOP Violence Against Women Act
Herbert Terry
Phone: (601) 359-7880
Fax: (601) 359-7832

VOCA Victim Assistance
Ezzard Charles Stamps
Phone: (601) 987-3978
Fax: (601) 987-4154
Psafety@dps.state.ms.us

VOCA Victim Compensation
Sandra Morrison
Phone: (601) 359-6766
Fax: (601) 359-3262
morriss@dfa.state.ms.us

Children's Justice Act
Mike Lee
Phone: (601) 359-4512
Fax: (601) 359-4333
mlee@mdhs.state.ms.us

Office for State and Local Domestic Preparedness Support
Richard Webster
Phone: (601) 960-9969
Fax: (601) 352-8314
rwebster@memaorg.com

MISSOURI

Edward Byrne Formula Grant
Patricia Rellergert
Phone: (573) 751-5997
Fax: (573) 751-5399
patty@dps.state.mo.us

Family Violence Prevention and Services Act
Dirk Elrod
Phone: (573) 751-2075
Fax: (573) 526-3971

STOP Violence Against Women Act
Vicky Scott
Phone: (573) 751-4905
Fax: (573) 751-5399

VOCA Victim Assistance
Vicky Scott
Phone: (573) 751-4905
Fax: (573) 751-5399
vscott@mail.state.mo.us

VOCA Victim Compensation
Susan Sudduth
Phone: (573) 526-3511
Fax: (573) 526-4940
ssudduth@central.dolir.state.mo.us

Children's Justice Act
Theresa Chester
Phone: (573) 751-8932
Fax: (573) 526-3971
tchester@mail.state.mo.us

Office for State and Local Domestic Preparedness Support
Jerry Uhlmann
Phone: (573) 526-9101
Fax: (573) 634-7966
juhlmann@mail.state.mo.us

MONTANA

Edward Byrne Formula Grant
Al Brockway
Phone: (406) 444-3604
Fax: (406) 444-4722
abrockway@state.mt.us

Family Violence Prevention and Services Act
Bette Hall
Phone: (406) 444-5903
Fax: (406) 444-5956
bhall@state.mt.us

STOP Violence Against Women Act
Nancy Knight
Phone: (406) 444-1995
Fax: (406) 444-4722

VOCA Victim Assistance
Nancy Knight
Phone: (406) 444-3604
Fax: (406) 444-4722
nknight@state.mt.us

VOCA Victim Compensation
Kathy Matson
Phone: (406) 444-3653
Fax: (406) 444-4722
kmatson@state.mt.us

Children's Justice Act
Bette Hall
Phone: (406) 444-5903
Fax: (406) 444-5956
bhall@state.mt.us

Office for State and Local Domestic Preparedness Support
James Greene
Phone: (406) 841-3911
Fax: (406) 841-3965
jigreeme@state.mt.us

NEBRASKA

Edward Byrne Formula Grant
Nancy Steeves
Phone: (402) 471-3416
Fax: (402) 471-2837

Family Violence Prevention and Services Act
Chris Hanus
Phone: (402) 471-9106
Fax: (402) 471-9455

STOP Violence Against Women Act
LaVonna Evans
Phone: (402) 471-2194
Fax: (402) 471-2837

VOCA Victim Assistance
LaVonna Evans
Phone: (402) 271-2194
Fax: (402) 471-2837
levans@crimecom.state.ne.us

VOCA Victim Compensation
Nancy Steeves
Phone: (402) 471-2194
Fax: (402) 471-2837
nSteeves@crimecom.state.ne.us

Children's Justice Act
Margaret Bitz
Phone: (402) 471-9457
Fax: (402) 471-9034
Margaret.bitz@hhss.state.ne.us

Office for State and Local Domestic Preparedness Support
Al Brendt
Phone: (402) 471-7410
Fax: (402) 471-7433
Al.berndt@nema.state.ne.us

NEVADA

Edward Byrne Formula Grant
Sandra Mazy
Phone: (775) 687-5282
Fax: (775) 687-6328

Family Violence Prevention and Services Act
Chris Graham
Phone: (775) 688-1628
Fax: (775) 688-1616
cgraham@govmail.state.nv.us

STOP Violence Against Women Act
Frankie Sue Del Papa
Phone: (775) 684-1100
Fax: (702) 684-1108

VOCA Victim Assistance
Chris Graham
Phone: (775) 688-1673
Fax: (775) 688-1616
Cgraham@govmail.state.nv.us

VOCA Victim Compensation
Patricia Moore
Phone: (702) 486-2740
Fax: (702) 486-2555
George Crown
Phone: (702) 688-2900

Children's Justice Act
Marjorie Walker
Phone: (775) 684-4422
Fax: (775) 684-4456
mwalker@govmail.state.nv.us

Office for State and Local Domestic Preparedness Support
Gary Derks
Phone: (775) 687-7380
Fax: (775) 687-8702
Gsd@quick.com

NEW HAMPSHIRE

Edward Byrne Formula Grant
Gale Dean
Phone: (603) 271-7987
Fax: (603) 271-2110

Family Violence Prevention and Services Act
Bernise Bluhm
Phone: (603) 271-4440
Fax: (603) 271-4729
bbluhm@dhhs.state.nh.us

STOP Violence Against Women Act
Mark C. Thompson
Phone: (603) 271-1234
Fax: (603) 271-2110

VOCA Victim Assistance
Gale Dean
Phone: (603) 271-7987
Fax: (603) 271-2110
gdean@doj.state.nh.us

VOCA Victim Compensation
Kim Therrien
Phone: (603) 271-1284
Fax: (603) 271-2110
ktherrien@doj.state.nh.us

Children's Justice Act
Sandra Matheson
Phone: (603) 271-3671
Fax: (603) 271-2110
smatheson@doj.state.nh.us

Office for State and Local Domestic Preparedness Support
Timothy Brackett
Phone: (603) 271-8090
Fax: (603) 271-2110
Tbrackett@doj.state.nh.us

NEW JERSEY

Edward Byrne Formula Grant
Heddy Levine-Sabol
Phone: (609) 292-1502
Fax: (609) 292-1451

Family Violence Prevention and Services Act
Karen Beckmeyer
Phone: (609) 984-8201
Fax: (609) 984-0509

STOP Violence Against Women Act
Theresa Martinac
Phone: (609) 588-6475
Fax: (609) 588-7890

VOCA Victim Assistance
Theresa Martinac
Phone: (609) 588-4698
Fax: (609) 588-7890
martinact@smtp.lps.state.nj.us

VOCA Victim Compensation
Jim Casserly
Phone: (973) 648-2107 x7716
Fax: (973) 648-7031
jamescasserly@excite.com

Children's Justice Act
Donna Pincavage
Phone: (609) 292-0888
Fax: (609) 633-2926
dpincavag@dhs.state.nj.us

Office for State and Local Domestic Preparedness Support
Steven Talpas
Phone: (609) 984-0634
Fax: (609) 292-3508
Steven.talpas@lps.state.nj.us

<u>NEW MEXICO</u>

Edward Byrne Formula Grant
Thomas Montoya
Phone: (505) 827-3427
Fax: (505) 827-3398

Family Violence Prevention and Services Act
Aurtie Tortorici
Phone: (505) 827-8067

STOP Violence Against Women Act
Larry Tackman
Phone: (505) 841-9432
Fax: (505) 841-9437

VOCA Victim Assistance
Robin Brassie
Phone: (505) 841-9432
Fax: (505) 841-9437
Robin.brassie@state.mn.us

VOCA Victim Compensation
Larry Tackman
Phone: (505) 841-9432
Fax: (505) 841-9437
Larry.tackman@state.mn.us

Children's Justice Act
Richard Lindahl
Phone: (505) 827-7625
Fax: (505) 827-8408
RGLINDAHL@cyfd.state.nm.us

Office for State and Local Domestic Preparedness Support
Michael Brown
Phone: (505) 476-9606
Fax: (505) 471-9650
erodriguez@dps.state.nm.us

NEW YORK

Edward Byrne Formula Grant
Gary Schreivogl
Phone: (518) 457-8462
Fax: (518) 457-1186

Family Violence Prevention and Services Act
Saleika Leak
Phone: (518) 473-6239

STOP Violence Against Women Act
Margaret Chretien
Phone: (518) 485-9607
Fax: (518) 485-8357

VOCA Victim Assistance
Anne Marie Strano
Phone: (518) 457-1779
Fax: (518) 457-8658
amstrano@nysnet.net

VOCA Victim Compensation
Jennifer Pirrone
Phone: (518) 457-8003
Fax: (518) 457-8658
jpirrone@nysnet.net

Children's Justice Act
Thomas Hess
Phone: (518) 474-4086
Fax: (518) 402-6824
89A794@dfa.state.ny.us

Office for State and Local Domestic Preparedness Support
Gary Schreivogl
Phone: (518) 457-8462
Fax: (518) 457-1186
schreivogl@dcjs.state.ny.us

NORTH CAROLINA

Edward Byrne Formula Grant
Craig Turner
Phone: (919) 733-4564
Fax: (919) 733-4625

Family Violence Prevention and Services Act
Alice Coleman
Phone: (919) 733-3677
Fax: (919) 715-0023

STOP Violence Against Women Act
Barry Bryant
Phone: (919) 733-4564
Fax: (919) 733-4625

VOCA Victim Assistance
Barry Bryant
Phone: (919) 733-4564
Fax: (919) 733-4625
Barry.Bryant@ncmail.net

VOCA Victim Compensation
Robert Reives
Phone: (919) 733-7974
Fax: (919) 715-4209
rreives@nccrimecontrol.org

Children's Justice Act
Joel Rosch
Phone: (919) 733-4564
Fax: (919) 733-4625
Joel.rosch@ncmail.net

Office for State and Local Domestic Preparedness Support
Eric Tolbert
Phone: (919) 733-3825
Fax: (919) 733-5406
etolbert@ncem.org

NORTH DAKOTA

Edward Byrne Formula Grant
Tammy Becker
Phone: (701) 328-5500
Fax: (701) 328-5510
Msmail.Tbecker@ranch.state.ND.US

Family Violence Prevention and Services Act
Mary Dasovick
Phone: (701) 328-3340
Fax: (701) 328-1412

STOP Violence Against Women Act
Mary Dasovick
Phone: (701) 328-3340
Fax: (701) 328-1412

VOCA Victim Assistance
Paul Coughlin
Phone: (701) 328-6195
Fax: (701) 328-6651
pcoughli@state.nd.us

VOCA Victim Compensation
Paul Coughlin
Phone: (701) 328-6295
Fax: (701) 328-6651
pcoughli@state.nd.us

Children's Justice Act
Gladys Cairns
Phone: (701) 328-4806
Fax: (701) 328-3538
socaig@state.nd.us

Office for State and Local Domestic Preparedness Support
Douglas Friez
Phone: (701) 328-8102
Fax: (701) 328-8181
dfriez@state.nd.us

OHIO

Edward Byrne Formula Grant
Venita Butler
Phone: (614) 466-7782
Fax: (614) 466-0308
webb@ocjs.state.oh.us

Family Violence Prevention and Services Act
Erika Taylor
Phone: (614) 752-6248
Fax: (614) 466-0164

STOP Violence Against Women Act
Stephanie Graubner
Phone: (614) 728-8738
Fax: (614) 466-0308

VOCA Victim Assistance
Sharon Boyer
Phone: (614) 466-5610
Fax: (614) 752-2732
wboyer@ag.state.oh.us

VOCA Victim Compensation
Brian Cook
Phone: (614) 466-5610
Fax: (614) 752-2732
bcook@ag.state.oh.us

Children's Justice Act
Kristin Gilbert
Phone: (614) 466-9824
Fax: (614) 466-0164
gilbek@odjfs.state.oh.us

Office for State and Local Domestic Preparedness Support
James Williams
Phone: (614) 889-7150
Fax: (614) 889-7183
Jwilliams@dps.state.oh.us

OKLAHOMA

Edward Byrne Formula Grant
Louietta Jones
Phone: (405) 264-5008
Fax: (405) 264-5095

Family Violence Prevention and Services Act
Ann Lowrance
Phone: (405) 522-3862
Fax: (405) 522-3650

STOP Violence Against Women Act
Louietta Jones
Phone: (405) 264-5008
Fax: (405) 264-5095

VOCA Victim Assistance
Susanne Breedlove
Phone: 1-800-745-6098
Fax: (405) 264-5097
breedlos@dac.state.ok.us

VOCA Victim Compensation
Susanne Breedlove
Phone: (405) 264-5006
Fax: (405) 264-5097
breedlos@dac.state.ok.us

Children's Justice Act
Kathryn Simms
Phone: (405) 521-2283
Fax: (405) 521-4373
Kathy.simms@okdhs.org

Office for State and Local Domestic Preparedness Support
B. W. Walker
Phone: (405) 425-2001
Fax: (405) 425-2324
bwwalker@dps.state.ok.us

OREGON

Edward Byrne Formula Grant
Carmen Merlo
Phone: (503) 378-3725 ext. 4145
Fax: (503) 378-6993
Carmen.Merlo@state.oh.us

Family Violence Prevention and Services Act
Bonnie J. Braeutigam
Phone: (503) 945-6686
Fax: (503) 581-6198

STOP Violence Against Women Act
Renee Kim
Phone: (503) 378-3725
Fax: (503) 378-6993

VOCA Victim Assistance
Connie Gallagher
Phone: (503) 378-5348
Fax: (503) 378-5738
Connie.Gallagher@doj.state.or.us

VOCA Victim Compensation
Connie Gallagher
Phone: (503) 378-5348
Fax: (503) 378-5738

Children's Justice Act
Sharon Bolen
Phone: (503) 945-5690
Fax: (503) 581-6198
Sharon.bolen@state.or.us

Office for State and Local Domestic Preparedness Support
Carmen Merlo
Phone: (503) 378-3720
Fax: (503) 378-6993
Carmen.merlo@state.or.us

PENNSYLVANIA

Edward Byrne Formula Grant
Bob Donovan
Phone: (717) 787-8559
Fax: (717) 772-0551
Donovan@pccd.state.pa.us

Family Violence Prevention and Services Act
Catherine Kimmel
Phone: (717) 787-7408
Fax: (717) 772-2093

STOP Violence Against Women Act
Michael Pennington
Phone: (717) 783-0551
Fax: (717) 772-7331

VOCA Victim Assistance
Michael Pennington
Phone: (717) 787-8559 x3031
Fax: (717) 783-7713

VOCA Victim Compensation
Carol Lavery
Phone: (717) 783-0551 x3215
Fax: (717) 783-7713
lavery@pccd.state.pa.us

Office for State and Local Domestic Preparedness Support
Mimi Myslewicz
Phone: (717) 651-2020
Fax: (717) 651-2025
mimyslezic@state.pa.us

RHODE ISLAND

Edward Byrne Formula Grant
David LeDoux
Phone: (401) 222-4495
Fax: (401) 277-1294

Family Violence Prevention and Services Act
Gail Dunphy
Phone: (401) 462-6865
Fax: (401) 464-1876

STOP Violence Against Women Act
Kirsten Martineau
Phone: (401) 222-5349
Fax: (401) 222-1294

VOCA Victim Assistance
Joseph L. Persia
Phone: (401) 277-4498
Fax: (401) 277-1294
joep@gw.doa.state.ri.us

VOCA Victim Compensation
Catherine King Avila
Phone: (401) 277-2287
Fax: (401) 222-2212
Cavila@treasury.state.ri.us

Children's Justice Act
C. Lee Baker
Phone: (401) 528-3794
Fax: (401) 528-3760
baker@dcyf.state.ri.us

Office for State and Local Domestic Preparedness Support
John Aucott
Phone: (401) 462-7127
Fax: (401) 944-1891
John.aucott@ri.ngb.army.mil

SOUTH CAROLINA

Edward Byrne Formula Grant
Ginger Dukes
Phone: (803) 896-8706
Fax: (803) 896-8714
dukesm@scdps.state.sc.us

Family Violence Prevention and Services Act
Valerie Doughty
Phone: (803) 898-7504
Fax: (803) 734-6285
vdoughty@dss.state.sc.us

STOP Violence Against Women Act
Barbara Jean Nelson
Phone: (803) 896-8712
Fax: (803) 896-8714

VOCA Victim Assistance
Barbara Jean Nelson
Phone: (803) 896-7896
Fax: (803) 896-8714
Nelson_Barbara@scdps.state.sc.us

VOCA Victim Compensation
Renee Graham
Phone: (803) 734-1930
Fax: (803) 734-1708
rgraham@govepp.state.ri.us

Children's Justice Act
S. Elizabeth Williams
Phone: (803) 898-7514
Fax: (803) 898-7641
bwilliams@dss.state.sc.us

Office for State and Local Domestic Preparedness Support
Stanley McKinney
Phone: (803) 737-8500
Fax: (803) 737-8570
smmckinn@strider.epd.state.sc.us

SOUTH DAKOTA

Edward Byrne Formula Grant
Wanda L. Fergen
Phone: (605) 773-6313
Fax: (605) 773-6471

Family Violence Prevention and Services Act
Susan Sheppick
Phone: (605) 773-4330
Fax: (605) 773-4855

STOP Violence Against Women Act
Susan Sheppick
Phone: (605) 773-4330
Fax: (605) 773-6834

VOCA Victim Assistance
Susan Sheppick
Phone: (605) 773-4330
Fax: (605) 773-6834
susans@dss.state.sd.us

VOCA Victim Compensation
Ann Holzhauser
Phone: (605) 773-6317
Fax: (605) 773-6834
Ann.holzhauser@state.sd.us

Children's Justice Act
Merlin Weyer
Phone: (605) 773-3227
Fax: (605) 773-6834
Merlin.weyer@state.sd.us

Office for State and Local Domestic Preparedness Support
John Berheim
Phone: (605) 773-3231
Fax: (605) 773-3580
John.berheim@state.sd.us

TENNESSEE

Edward Byrne Formula Grant
Patricia B. Dishman
Phone: (615) 741-8277
Fax: (615) 532-2989
pdishman@mail.state.tn.us

Family Violence Prevention and Services Act
Dora Hemphill
Phone: (615) 253-1983
Fax: (615) 532-9956

STOP Violence Against Women Act
Terry Hweitt
Phone: (615) 532-3355
Fax: (615) 532-2989

VOCA Victim Assistance
Terry Hweitt
Phone: (615) 532-3355
Fax: (615) 532-2989
Thewitt2@mail.state.tn.us

VOCA Victim Compensation
Amy Dunlap
Phone: (615) 741-2734
Fax: (615) 532-4979
adunlap@mail.state.tn.us

Children's Justice Act
Vickie Lawson
Phone: (615) 532-5622
Fax: (615) 532-6495
vrlawson@mail.state.tn.us

Office for State and Local Domestic Preparedness Support
Stan Copeland
Phone: (615) 741-9742
Fax: (615) 741-4173
scopeland@tnema.org

TEXAS

Edward Byrne Formula Grant
Robert J. Bodisch, Sr.
Phone: (512) 463-1806
Fax: (512) 475-2440

Family Violence Prevention and Services Act
Liz Cruz Garbett
Phone: (512) 438-5440

STOP Violence Against Women Act
Amiee Snoddy
Phone: (512) 463-1924
Fax: (512) 475-2440

VOCA Victim Assistance
Nancy Carrales
Phone: (512) 463-1944
Fax: (512) 475-2440
ncarrales@governor.state.tx.us

VOCA Victim Compensation
Rex Uberman
Phone: (512) 936-1200
Fax: (512) 320-8270
Rex.uberman@oag.state.tx.us

Children's Justice Act
Rebecca Faith Jones
Phone: (512) 908-4550
Fax: (512) 908-4554
jonesrf@tdprs.state.tx.us

Office for State and Local Domestic Preparedness Support
Charlie Todd
Phone: (409) 458-6815
Fax: (409) 458-6810
Kem.Bennett@texmail.tamu.edu

UTAH

Edward Byrne Formula Grant
Marvin Dodge
Phone: (801) 538-1031
Fax: (801) 538-1024
mododge@state.ut.us

Family Violence Prevention and Services Act
Duane Betournay
Phone: (801) 538-4526
Fax: (801) 538-3993

STOP Violence Against Women Act
Christine Watters
Phone: (801) 238-2360
Fax: (801) 533-4127

VOCA Victim Assistance
Christine Watters
Phone: (801) 238-2360
Fax: (801) 533-4127
cwatters@gov.state.ut.us

VOCA Victim Compensation
Dan R. Davis
Phone: (801) 238-2360
Fax: (801) 533-4127
Ddavis@gov.state.ut.us

Children's Justice Act
Brenda George
Phone: (801) 538-1944
Fax: (801) 538-1699
Atcap01.bgeroge@state.ut.us

Office for State and Local Domestic Preparedness Support
John Rokich
Phone: (801) 538-3788
Fax: (801) 538-3770
jrokich@dps.state.ut.us

VERMONT

Edward Byrne Formula Grant
Capt. A. Marc Metayer
Phone: (802) 241-5272
Fax: (802) 241-5551

Family Violence Prevention and Services Act
Lori Hayes
Phone: (802) 241-1250
Fax: (802) 241-1253
lhayes@ccvs.state.vt.us

STOP Violence Against Women Act
Lori Hayes
Phone: (802) 241-1250
Fax: (802) 241-1253

VOCA Victim Assistance
Judy Rex
Phone: (802) 241-1250
Fax: (802) 241-1253
jrex@ccvs.state.vt.us

VOCA Victim Compensation
Lori Hayes
Phone: (802) 241-1250
Fax: (802) 241-1253
lhayes@ccvs.state.vt.us

Children's Justice Act
Stacey Edmunds
Phone: (802) 863-7569
Fax: (802) 651-1662
sedmunds@srs.state.vt.us

Office for State and Local Domestic Preparedness Support
Robert deMange
Phone: (802) 244-8721
Fax: (802) 244-8655
evonturk@dps.state.vt.us

VIRGINIA

Edward Byrne Formula Grant
Janice Waddy
Phone: (804) 786-1577
Fax: (804) 371-8981

Family Violence Prevention and Services Act
Sonia Rivero
Phone: (804) 692-1900
Fax: (804) 692-1949
Hsus300@dshs.wa.gov

STOP Violence Against Women Act
Mandi Patterson
Phone: (804) 786-3923
Fax: (804) 371-8981

VOCA Victim Assistance
Mandie Patterson
Phone: (804) 786-3923
Fax: (804) 786-7980
Mpatterson.dcjs@state.va.us

VOCA Victim Compensation
William Dudley
Phone: (804) 378-4371
Fax: (804) 367-9740
William.Dudley@vwc.state.va.us

Children's Justice Act
Holly S. Oehrlein
Phone: (804) 371-0534
Fax: (804) 786-3414
hoehrlein@dcjs.state.va.us

Office for State and Local Domestic Preparedness Support
George Foresman
Phone: (804) 897-6580
Fax: (804) 897-6506
Gforesman.des@state.va.us

WASHINGTON

Edward Byrne Formula Grant
Paul Perz
Phone: (360) 586-8411
Fax: (360) 586-0489
paulp@cted.wa.gov

Family Violence Prevention and Services Act
Susan Hannibal
Phone: (206) 923-4910
Fax: (206) 923-4899

STOP Violence Against Women Act
Anita Granbois
Phone: (360) 753-4934
Fax: (260) 586-7176

VOCA Victim Assistance
Susan Hannibal
Phone: (206) 923-4910
Fax: (360) 902-7903
Hsus300@dshs.wa.gov

VOCA Victim Compensation
Cletus Nnanabu
Phone: (360) 902-5340
Fax: (360) 902-5333
Nnan235@lni.wa.gov

Children's Justice Act
Caroline Ford
Phone: (360) 902-7996
Fax: (360) 902-7903
Foca300@dshs.wa.gov

Office for State and Local Domestic Preparedness Support
Glen Woodbury
Phone: (253) 512-7001
Fax: (253) 512-7207
g.woodbury@emd.wa.gov

WEST VIRGINIA

Edward Byrne Formula Grant
Mike Cutlip
Phone: (304) 558-8814 x206
Fax: (304) 558-0391

Family Violence Prevention and Services Act
Diane Crump
Phone: (304) 288-7980
Fax: (304) 288-8800

STOP Violence Against Women Act
Tonia Thomas
Phone: (304) 558-8814 x216
Fax: (304) 558-0391

VOCA Victim Assistance
Tonia Thomas
Phone: (304) 558-8814 x216
Fax: (304) 558-0391
Tthomas1@wvdcjs.state.wv.us

VOCA Victim Compensation
John Fulks
Phone: (304) 347-4851
Fax: (304) 347-4915
jfederspiel@wvdcjs.org

Children's Justice Act
Kathie King
Phone: (304) 558-7980
Fax: (304) 558-8800
kking@wvdhhr.org

Office for State and Local Domestic Preparedness Support
John Pack, Jr.
Phone: (304) 558-5380
Fax: (304) 334-4538
Jpack1@wvoes.state.wv.us

WISCONSIN

Edward Byrne Formula Grant
Stephen Grohmann
Phone: (608) 266-7185
Fax: (608) 266-6676

Family Violence Prevention and Services Act
Martha Mallon
Phone: (608) 266-6305

STOP Violence Against Women Act
Kittie Smith
Phone: (608) 261-8762
Fax: (608) 266-6676

VOCA Victim Assistance
Kitty Kocol
Phone: (608) 267-2221
Fax: (608) 264-6368

VOCA Victim Compensation
Gretchen MacDonald
Phone: (608) 266-6470
Fax: (608) 264-6368
macdonaldsgi@doj.state.wi.us

Children's Justice Act
Ann Rulseh
Phone: (608) 266-3934
Fax: (608) 264-6368
rulseham@doj.state.wi.us

Office for State and Local Domestic Preparedness Support
Christine Bacon
Phone: (608) 242-3206
Fax: (608) 242-3249
baconc@dma.state.wi.us

WYOMING

Edward Byrne Formula Grant
Jennifer Wroe
Phone: (307) 777-6785
Fax: (307) 777-6869
jwroe@state.wy.us

Family Violence Prevention and Services Act
Nancy Dawson
Phone: (307) 777-7200
Fax: (307) 777-6683

STOP Violence Against Women Act
Sharon Montagnino
Phone: (307) 777-7841
Fax: (307) 777-6683

VOCA Victim Assistance
Sharon Montagnino
Phone: (307) 777-6515
Fax: (307) 777-6683
smonta@missc.state.wy.us

VOCA Victim Compensation
Sharon Montagnino
Phone: (307) 777-7200
Fax: (307) 777-6683
smonta@missc.state.wy.us

Children's Justice Act
Steven Vajda
Phone: (307) 777-6081
Fax: (307) 777-3693
svajda@state.wy.us

Office for State and Local Domestic Preparedness Support
Dr. John Heller
Phone: (307) 777-4912
Fax: (307) 635-6017   36
hellerj@wy-arng.ngb.army.mil

CHAPTER TWENTY

DIRECTORY OF
VICTIM ASSISTANCE PROGRAMS

CHAPTER TWENTY
DIRECTORY OF VICTIM ASSISTANCE PROGRAMS

This chapter was designed to inform the students of the Victim Assistance Programs within the United States of America. The subsequent directory commences with the State of Alabama and ends with the State of Wyoming. The Victim Assistance Programs have been situated within the District Attorney(s) or the Prosecutor's Office.

ALABAMA

15th Judicial Circuit
Montgomery
Ellen Brooks
District Attorney
251 S Lawrence St
Montgomery 36102
334-832-2550

ALASKA

First Judicial District
Richard A. Svobodny
District Attorney
P.O. Box 110300
Juneau 99811
907-465-3620

ARIZONA

Maricopa County
Richard M. Romley
County Attorney
301 W Jefferson St Ste 800
Phoenix 85003
602-506-3411

ARKANSAS

6th Judicial District
Perry, Pulaski
Larry Jegley
Prosecuting Attorney
122 S Broadway St
Little Rock 72201
501-340-8000

CALIFORNIA

Sacramento County
Jan Scully
District Attorney
901 G St
Sacramento 95814
916-874-6218

COLORADO

2nd Judicial District
Denver
A. William Ritter Jr.
District Attorney
303 W Colfax Ave Ste 1300
Denver 80204
720-913-9000

CONNECTICUT

Hartford Judicial District
Avon, Bloomfield, Canton, East Granby, East Hartford, East Windsor, Enfield, Farmington, Glastonbury, Granby, Hartford, Manchester, Marlborough, Simsbury, South Windsor, Suffield, West Hartford, Windsor, Windsor Locks
James E. Thomas
State's Attorney
101 Lafayette St
Hartford 06106
860-566-3190

DELAWARE

Attorney General
M. Jane Brady
820 N. French St. 6th Fl
Wilmington, DE   19801
302-577-8338

FLORIDA

2nd Judicial Circuit
Franklin, Gadsden, Jefferson, Leon, Liberty, Wakulla
William N. Meggs
State's Attorney
Leon Cnty Cthse 301 S Monroe St
Tallahassee 32399
850-488-6701

GEORGIA

Atlanta Judicial Circuit
Fulton
Paul L. Howard Jr.
District Attorney
136 Pryor St SW 3rd Fl
Atlanta 30303
404-730-4979

HAWAII

Honolulu County
County/City
Peter Carlisle
Prosecuting Attorney
1060 Richards St
Honolulu 96813
808-527-6494

IDAHO

Ada County
4th Judicial District
Greg H. Bower
Prosecuting Attorney
602 W Idaho St
Boise 83702
208-364-2121

ILLINOIS

Sangamon County
7th Judicial District
John Schmidt
State's Attorney
200 S 9th St Rm 402
Springfield 62701
217-753-6690

INDIANA

19th Judicial Circuit
Marion
Scott C. Newman
Prosecuting Attorney
200 E Washington Ste 560
Indianapolis 46204
317-327-3522

IOWA

Polk County
5th Judicial District
John P. Sarcone
County Attorney
206 6th Ave 2nd Fl
Des Moines 50309
515-286-3737

KANSAS

3rd Judicial District
Shawnee
Robert Hecht
District Attorney
Cthse 200 E 7th Rm 214
Topeka 66603
785-233-8200

KENTUCKY

48th Judicial Circuit
Franklin
Larry Cleveland
Commonwealth Attorney
315 W Main St
Frankfort 40601
502-564-4741

LOUISIANA

19th Judicial District
East Baton Rouge
Doug Moreau
District Attorney
222 St Louis St 5th Fl
Baton Rouge 70802
225-389-3470

MAINE

Kennebec County
4th Prosecutorial District
David Crook
District Attorney
95 State St
Augusta 04330
207-623-1156

MARYLAND

Anne Arundel County
5th Judicial Circuit
Frank R. Weathersbee
State's Attorney
7 Church Cir Ste 200
Annapolis 21401
410-222-1740

MASSACHUSETTS

Suffolk County
Ralph C. Martin II
District Attorney
One Bulfinch Pl
Boston 02114
617-619-4000

MICHIGAN

30th Judicial Circuit
Ingham
Stuart J. Dunnings III
Prosecuting Attorney
303 W. Kalamazoo St
Lansing 48933
517-483-6108

MINNESOTA

2nd Judicial District
Ramsey
Susan Gaertner
County Attorney
50 W Kellog Blvd Ste 315
St. Paul 55102
651-266-3222

MISSISSIPPI

Hinds County
Malcolm Harrison
Jackson, 39201
601-948-5030

MISSOURI

19th Judicial Circuit
Cole
Richard Callahan
Prosecuting Attorney
311 E High St 3rd Fl
Jefferson City 65101
573-634-9180

MONTANA

Lewis & Clark County
1st Judicial District
Leo Gallagher
County Attorney
228 Broadway
Helena 59601
406-447-8221

NEBRASKA

Lancaster County
3rd Judicial District
Gary E. Lacey
County Attorney
575 S 10th St
Lincoln 68508
402-441-7321

NEVADA

Carson (City-County)
1st Judicial District
Noel S. Waters
District Attorney
885 E Musser Ste 2030C
Carson City 89701
775-887-2072

NEW HAMPSHIRE

Merrimack County
Michael T. Johnson
County Attorney
4 Court St Ste 1
Concord 03301
603-228-0529

NEW JERSEY

Mercer County
Daniel G. Giaquinto
County Prosecutor
209 S Broad St
Trenton 08608
609-989-6309

NEW MEXICO

1st Judicial District
Los Alamos, Rio Arriba, Santa Fe
Henry R. Valdez
District Attorney
327 Sandoval St
Santa Fe 87504
505-827-5000

NEW YORK

Albany County
3rd Judicial District
Paul A. Clyne
District Attorney
Cnty Cthse Rm 218
Albany 12207-518-487-5460

NORTH CAROLINA

10th Judicial District
Wake
C C Willoughby
District Attorney
316 Fayetteville St Mall
Raleigh 27602
919-755-4117

NORTH DAKOTA

Burleigh County
S Central Judicial District
Richard J. Riha
State's Attorney
Cthse 514 E Thayer Ave
Bismarck 58501
701-222-6672

OHIO

Franklin County
Ronald J. O'Brien
Prosecuting Attorney
369 S High St
Columbus 43215
614-462-3555

OKLAHOMA

7th Judicial District
Oklahoma
Robert H. Macy
District Attorney
320 Robert S Kerr Ave Ste 505
Oklahoma City 73102
405-713-1600

OREGON

Marion County
21st Judicial District
Dale W. Penn
District Attorney
555 Court St
Salem 97301
503-588-5222

PENNSYLVANIA

12th Judicial District
Dauphin
Edward M. Marsico Jr.
District Attorney
Front & Market St
Harrisburg 17101
717-255-2770

RHODE ISLAND

Attorney General
Sheldon Whitehouse
Attorney General
150 S Main St
Providence 02903
401-274-4400

SOUTH CAROLINA

5th Judicial Circuit
Kershaw, Richland
W. Barney Giese
Solicitor
P.O. Box 1987
Columbia 29202
803-748-4785

SOUTH DAKOTA

Hughes County
6th Judicial Circuit
Mark Smith
State's Attorney
104 E Capitol
Pierre 57501
605-773-7462

TENNESSEE

20th Judicial District
Davidson
Victor S. Johnson III
District Attorney General
Ste 500 Wash Sq 222 2nd Ave N
Nashville 37201
615-862-5500 X190

TEXAS

Travis County
Ronald Earle
District Attorney
509 W 11th Criminal Justice Ctr
Austin 78701
512-473-9400

Ken Oden
County Attorney
314 W 11th St
Austin 78701
512-473-9415

UTAH

Salt Lake County
3rd Judicial District
David Yocom
District Attorney
2001 S State St S3500
Salt Lake City 84190
801-468-3300

VERMONT

See individual county

VIRGINIA

14th Judicial District
Henrico
Wade A. Kizer
Commonwealth Attorney
4301 E Parham Rd
Richmond 23273
804-501-4218

WASHINGTON

Thurston County
Edward G. Holm
Prosecuting Attorney
2000 Lakeridge Dr SW Bldg 2
Olympia 98502
360-786-5540

WEST VIRGINIA

13th Judicial Circuit
Kanawha
Michael Clifford
Prosecuting Attorney
111 Court St 3rd Fl
Charleston 25301
304-357-0300 X9880

WISCONSIN

Dane County
5th Judicial District
Brian Blanchard
District Attorney
210 M L King Jr Blvd Rm 523
Madison 53709
608-266-4211

WYOMING

1st Judicial District
Laramie
Jon Forwood
District Attorney
310 W 19th Ste 200
Cheyenne 82002
307-633-4360 37

APPENDIX

LIST OF NATIONAL VICTIM AND
SURVIVOR INFORMATION CENTERS

APPENDIX

Adam Walsh Resource Center (re: Missing and Exploited Children)
www.missingkids.com

American Association for Protecting Children, a Division of the American Humane
Association
www.americanhumaine.org

American Bar Association, Center on Children and the Law and Criminal Justice Section,
Victim-Witness Project
www.abanet.org/child

American Indian Law Center
www.lawschool.unm.edu/ailc

Bureau of Justice Statistics
www.ojp.usdoj.gov/bjs/

Center for Disease Control and Prevention
www.cdc.gov/

Center for Peacemaking and Conflict Studies
www.fresno.edu/dept/pacs

Center for Restorative Justice and Peacemaking
Ssw.che.umn.edu/rjp/

Child Abuse Prevention Network
Child.cornell.edu

Child Help USA
Childhelpusa.org

Conflict Resource Education Network
www.crenet.org/

Federal Bureau of Investigation
www.fbi.gov

Homicide Research Working Group
www.icpsr.umich.edu/NACJD/HRWG/

Kempe National Center for Prevention and Treatment of Child Abuse and Neglect
www.kempecenter.org

Institute for the Study of Alternative Dispute Resolution
www.humboldt.edu/~isadr/

Mothers Against Drunk Driving
www.madd.org

National Association of Counsel for Children
www.naccchildlaw.org

National Association of Crime Victim Compensation Boards
www.ncvc.org

National Center on Elder Abuse
www.gwjapan.com/ncea

National Center for Missing and Exploited Children
www.missingkids.org

National Center for Prosecution of Child Abuse
www.ndaa-apri/apri/ncpca/index.html

National Center for Victims of Crime
www.ncvc.org

National Clearinghouse on Child Abuse and Neglect
www.calib.com/nccanch

National Clearinghouse on Marital and Date Rape
http://ncmdr.org

National Coalition Against Domestic Violence
www.ncadv.org

National Coalition Against Sexual Assault
www.ncasa.org

National Committee for Prevention of Child Abuse
www.preventchildabuse.org

National Crime Prevention Council
www.ncpc.org

National Criminal Justice Reference Service Justice Information Center
www.ncjrs.org

National Crime Victim Bar Association
www.victimbar.org/

National Crime Victim's Center (NCVC)
www.ncvc.org

National Crime Victims Research and Treatment Center
www.musc.edu/cvc/

National Indian Justice Center
www.nijc.indian.com

National Institute of Mental Health, Antisocial and Violent Behavior Branch
www.nimh.nih.gov

National Organization for Victim Assistance
www.try-nova.org/

National Self-Help Clearinghouse
www.selfhelpweb.org

National Victim's Constitutional Amendment Network
www.nvcan.org

Office for Victims of Crime (OVC) of the Office for Justice Programs (OJP)
www.ojp.usdoj.gov/ovc

Parents of Murdered Children
www.pomc.com

Rape, Abuse, and Incest National Network
www.rainn.org/

Sourcebook of Criminal Justice Statistics
www.albany.edu/sourcebook/

The Stalking Victim's Sanctuary
www.stalkingvictims.com

Survivors of Stalking
www.soshelp.org/

Victim-Offender Mediation Association
www.voma.org

Victim-Offender Reconciliation Programs
www.vorp.com

Violence Against Women Office of the OJP
www.ojp.usdoj.gov/vawo/welcome.html

Wadsworth Publishing Company
www.wadsworth.com

Wife Rape Information Page
www.wellesley.edu/WCW/project/mrape.html

World Society of Victimology
www.victimology.nl/

RESOURCES

About Elder Abuse, (1985)., Massachussetts, Channing L. Bete Co., Inc.

Andrews, Arelene Bowers., (1992), Victimization and Survivor Services, New York: Springer Publishing Co.

Child Abuse, (2000), Maricopa County Attorney's Office, Arizona.

Civil Justice For Victims of Crimes, (2001), Washington, D.C., National Crime Victim Bar Association.

Crime Clock., (1999), FBI Uniform Crime Report, Washington, D.C. U.S. Justice Department. (Bureau of Justice).

Crary, Donald., Church Abuse, Gloucester County Times, February 24, 2002. (p.3-8).

Doerner, William G., and Lab, Steven P., (1998) 2nd Gd., Victimology. Ohio: Anderson Publishing Co.

Glenn, Leigh (1997). Victim Rights. California: ABC-CILO, Inc.

Harris, Jerry L., (2001) Murder: A Handbook for Families of Murder Victims and People Who Assist Them., Texas: Office of the Governor, Criminal Justice Division of Texas.

Jerin, Robert, and Moriarty, Laura J., (1998)., Victimology Research., North Carolina: Carolina Academic Press.

Karman, Andrew., (2000), 4th ed., Crime Victims, California: Wadsworth/Thomson Learning.

New Directions from the Field: Victim Rights and Services for the 21st Century: (1998)., Washington, D.C.: U.S. Department of Justice.

Mariani, cliff., (1996)., Domestic Violence Survival Guide., New York: Looseleaf Law Publications, Inc.

National Directory of Law Enforcement Administrators (2000) Correctional Institutions and Related Agencies. Span Publishing , Inc.

OVC National Directory of Victim Assistance Funding Opportunities (2001), US Department of Justice,Washington, DC. (2001)

Sexual Assault., (2000). New Mexico Attorney General's Office, New Mexico.

Someone You Know Drinks and Drives., (1995) 3rd ed., Texas: MADD Victim Services.

Stalking., (2002) National Center for Victims of Crime. Washington, D.C. Bureau of Justice Statistics.

Stalking., (2000), Maricopa County Attorney's Office, Arizona.

Surviving the Crisis, (1995)., Texas MADD Victim Services.

Tatara, Toshio., (1996)., Elder Abuse: Washington, D.C., National Center on Elder Abuse.

Viano, Emilio., (1990)., The Victimology Handbook, New York: Garland Publishing, Inc.

NOTES

1. New Directions From the Field: Victim Rights and Services for the 21st Century, (1998) pp.9-25.

2. Glenn, Leigh; Victim Rights, (1997) p.13.

3. Ibid. p.16

4. Doerner, William G., and Lab, Steven P., Victimology, (1998) pp.23-31.

5. Crime Clock, (1999) Uniform Crime Report. p.1.

6. Ibid. p.2

7. Doerner, William G., and Lab, Steven P., Victimology. pp.69-71.

8. Karmen, Andrew, (2000); Crime Victims, pp.269-274.

9. Ibid. p.280.

10. Ibid. pp. 281-282.

11. Ibid. p. 282-283.

12. Ibid. p.287.

13. Ibid. p.292-293.

14. Doerner, William G., and Lab, Steven P., (1998) Victimology. p.75.

15. Karmen, Andrew, (2000), Crime Victims, p.293.

16. Doerner, William G. and Lab Steven P., (1998) Victimology, pp.198-202.

17. Ibid. pp.202-204.

18. Child Find of America, Inc. (1994), New York, Stranger Abduction. p.2.

19. Child Find of America, Inc. (1994), New York, Parental Abduction. p.3.

20. Child Abuse, (2000), Maricopa County Attorney's Office. p.3.

21. Doerner, William G., and Lab Steven P., (1998) Victimology. pp. 140-148.

22. Tapara, Toshio, Elder Abuse, (1996). pp.3-8.

23. Doerner, William G., and Lab, Steven P., (1998), Victimology. pp112-114

24. Ibid., pp.116-120.

25.Sexual Assault., (2000). New Mexico Attorney General's Office. pp.2-10.

26. Karmen, Andrew, (2000). Crime Victims. pp.239-254.

27. Stalking's (2000) Maricopa County Attorney General's Office. pp.2-44.

28. Stalking's (2001) National Center for Victims of Crime. Pp.2-8.

29. Someone You Know Drinks and Drives (1995). MADD Victim Service. pp.2-12.

30. Surviving The Crisis, (1995), Texas MADD Victim Services. Pp.3-5.

31. Karmen, Andrew, (2000), Crime Victims. pp.319-321.

32. Ibid. pp.324-326.

33. Ibid. pp.330

34. Crary, Donald, Church Abuse, February 24, 2002. p.8.

35. OVC (Office for Victims of Crime of United Stated Department of Justice, Washington, D.C. p.1-2 (Quick Look Web Site)

36. Ibid. p1-2 (Quick Look Web Site)

37. National Director of Law Enforcement Administrators (2000) pp.507-605.

INDEX

F

G

H

I

N

O

P

R

S

T

U

V

W